EASY PIANO

2014 GREATEST CHRISTIAN HITS

ARRANGED BY
CAROL TORNQUIST

CONTENTS

Produced by
Alfred Music
P.O. Box 10003
Van Nuys, CA 91410-0003
alfred.com

Printed in USA.

ISBN-10: 1-4706-1143-0
ISBN-13: 978-1-4706-1143-9

Cover photo:
High-rise building: © Shutterstock.com / Vladitto

ALL THE PEOPLE SAID AMEN

Words and Music by Matt Maher,
Paul Moak and Trevor Morgan
Arr. Carol Tornquist

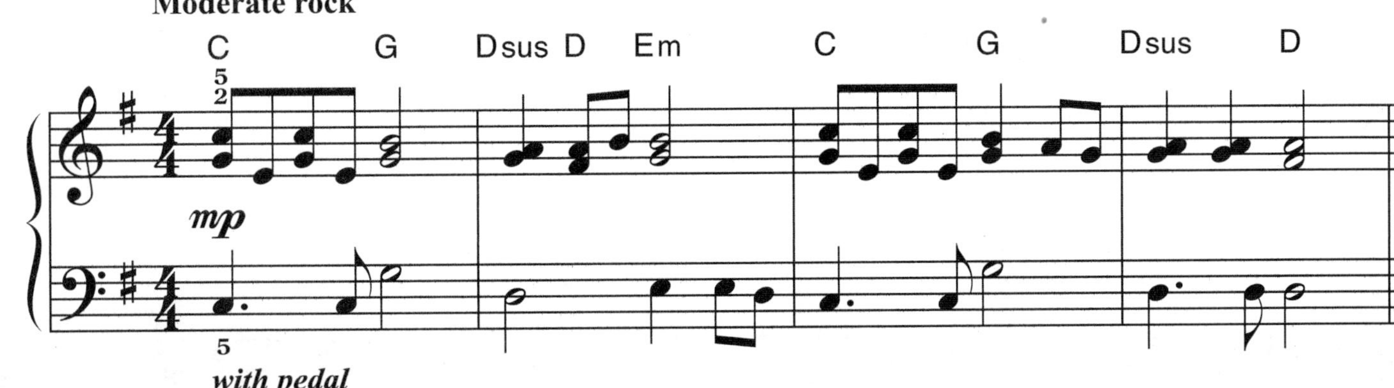

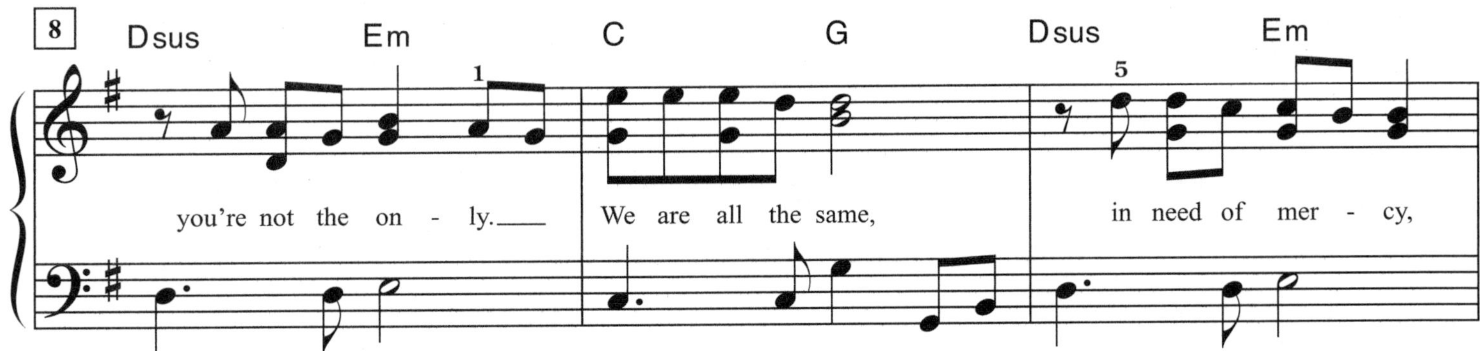

Chorus:
14
Dsus
D
G
D7
G
God, it's all you need.
mf
And all the peo-ple said, "A - men!" Whoa,

17
C
G
D
C
G
and all the peo-ple said, "A - men!" Give thanks to the Lord for His love

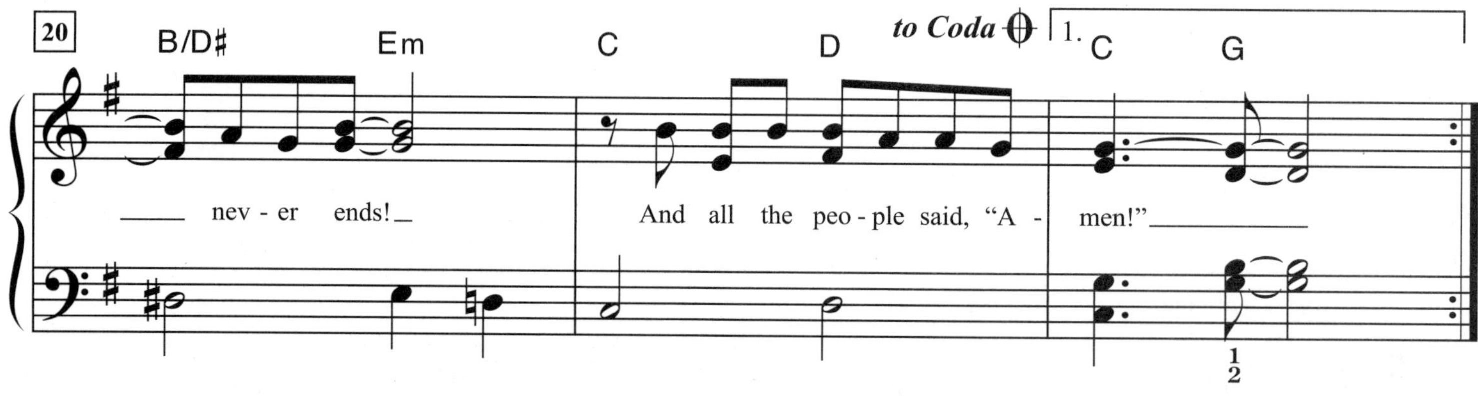
20
B/D♯
Em
C
D
to Coda
1.
C
G
nev - er ends!
And all the peo-ple said, "A - men!"

2.
Bridge:
23
C
G
C
G
D
Em
men!" Bless-ed are the poor in spir - it who are torn a - part. Bless-ed are

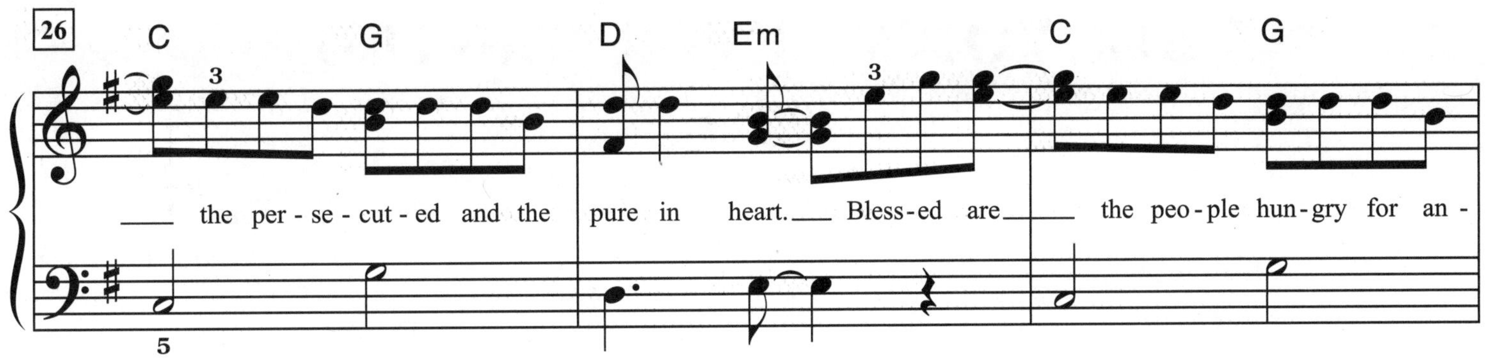

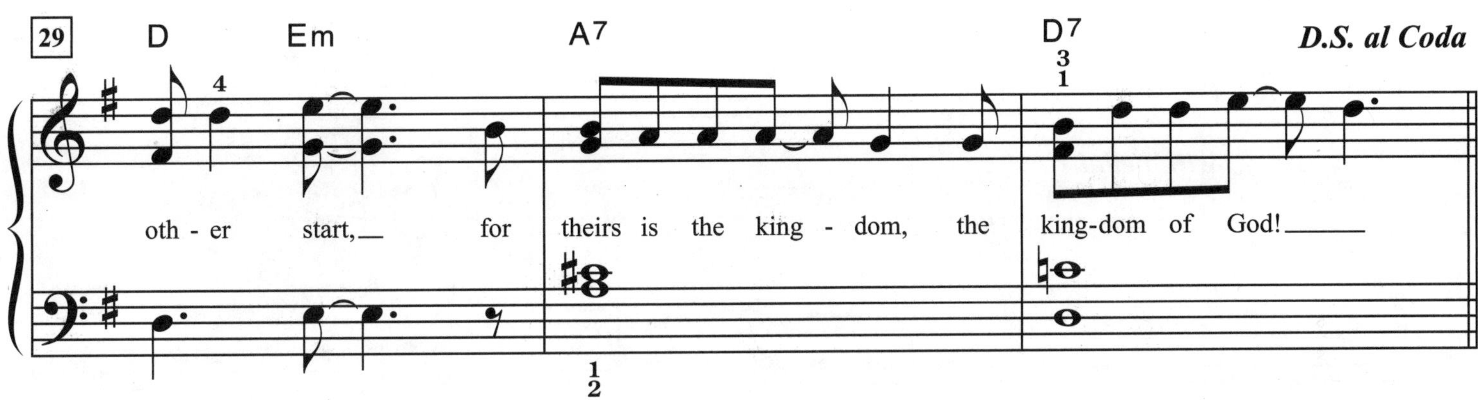

Verse 2:
If you're rich or poor, well, it don't matter.
Weak or strong, you know, love is what we're after.
We're all broken, but we're all in this together.
God knows we stumble and fall, and He so loved the world,
He sent His Son to save us all.

ALL YOU'VE EVER WANTED

Words and Music by
Bernie Herms and Mark Hall
Arr. Carol Tornquist

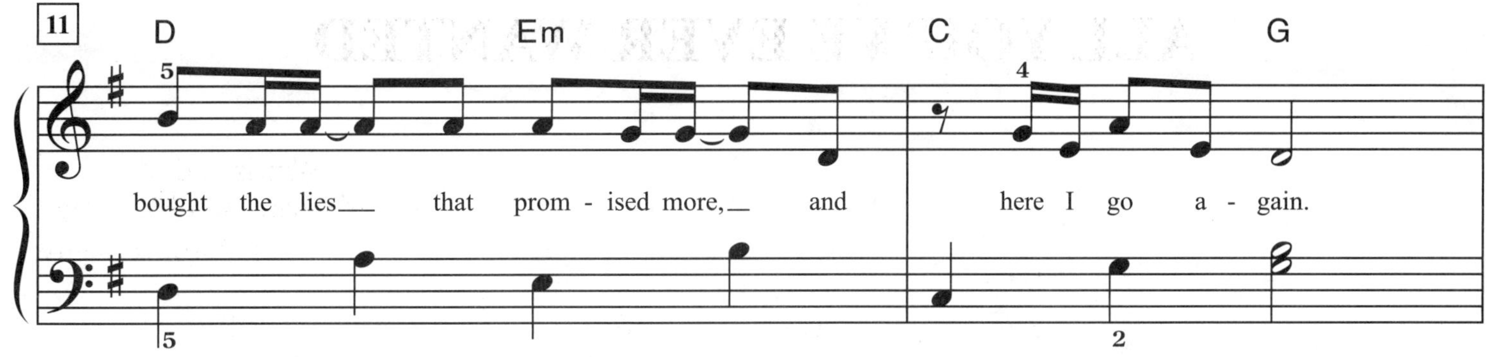
11
D
Em
C
G
bought the lies that prom - ised more, and
here I go a - gain.

13
D
Em
C
Oh.

15
D
Em
C
Oh.

Verse:
17
D
Em
C
G
2. Lord, I know I let You down, but
3. See additional lyrics.
some-how I will make You proud. I'll

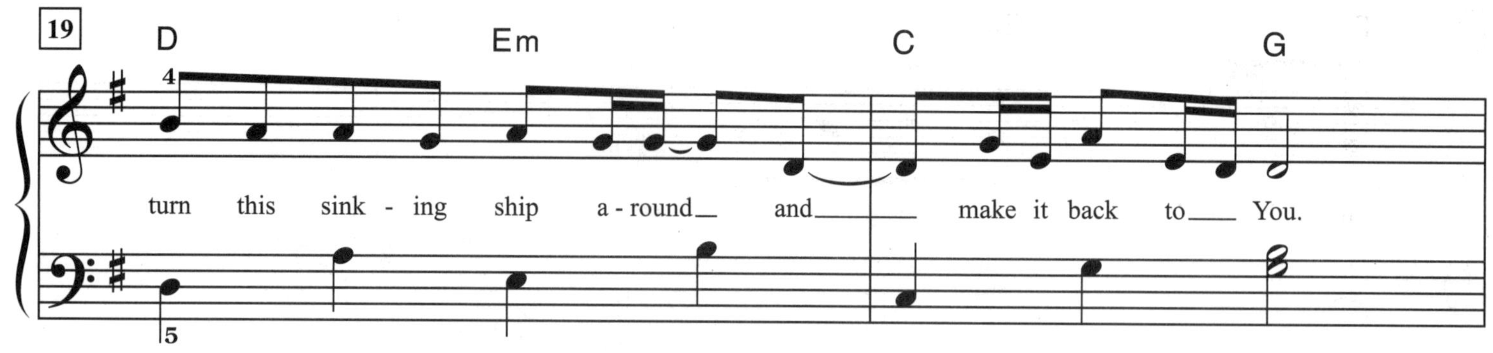
19
D
Em
C
G
turn this sink - ing ship a - round and make it back to You.

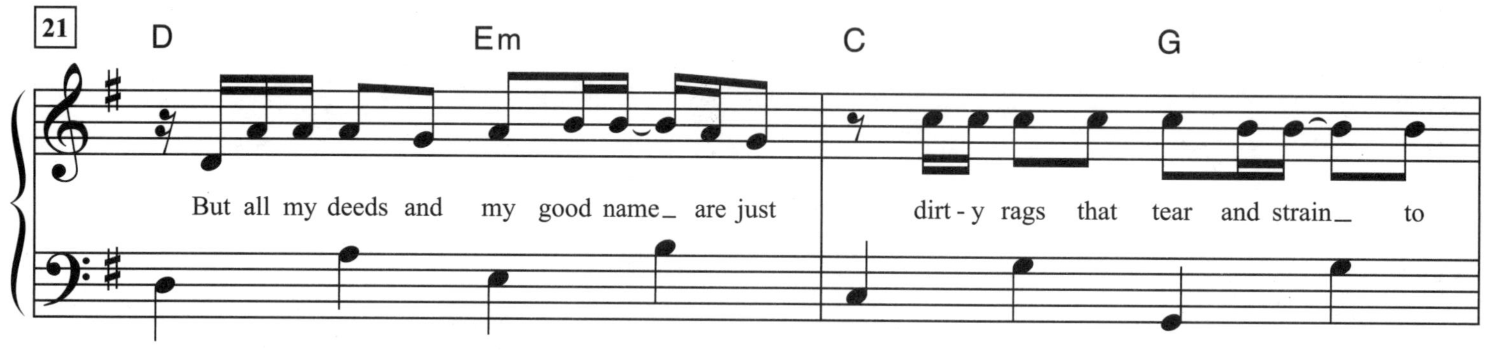
21
D
Em
C
G
But all my deeds and my good name are just dirt - y rags that tear and strain to

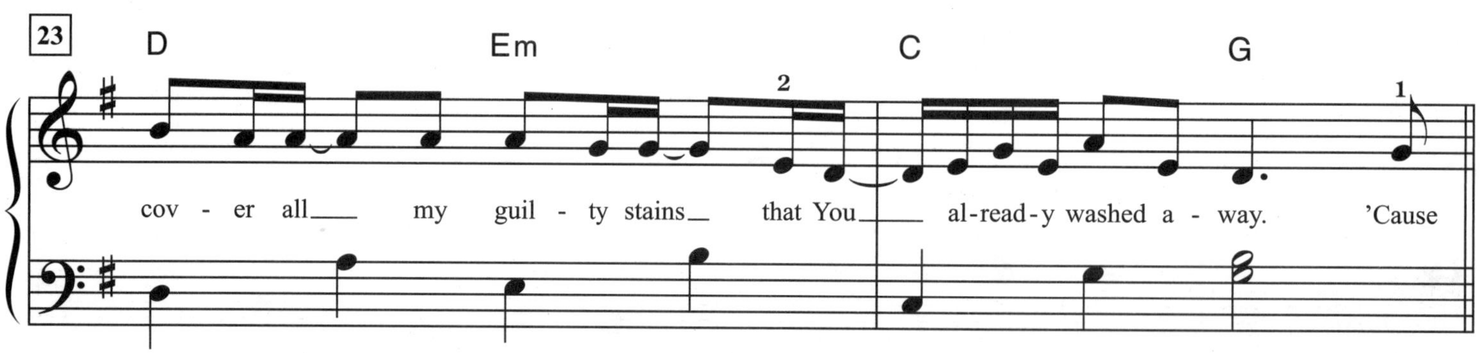
23
D
Em
C
G
cov - er all my guil - ty stains that You al - read - y washed a - way. 'Cause

Chorus:
25
D
Em7
C
G
mf
all You've ev - er want - ed,
all You've ev - er want - ed,

27
D
Em
C
G
all You've ev - er want - ed was my
heart.

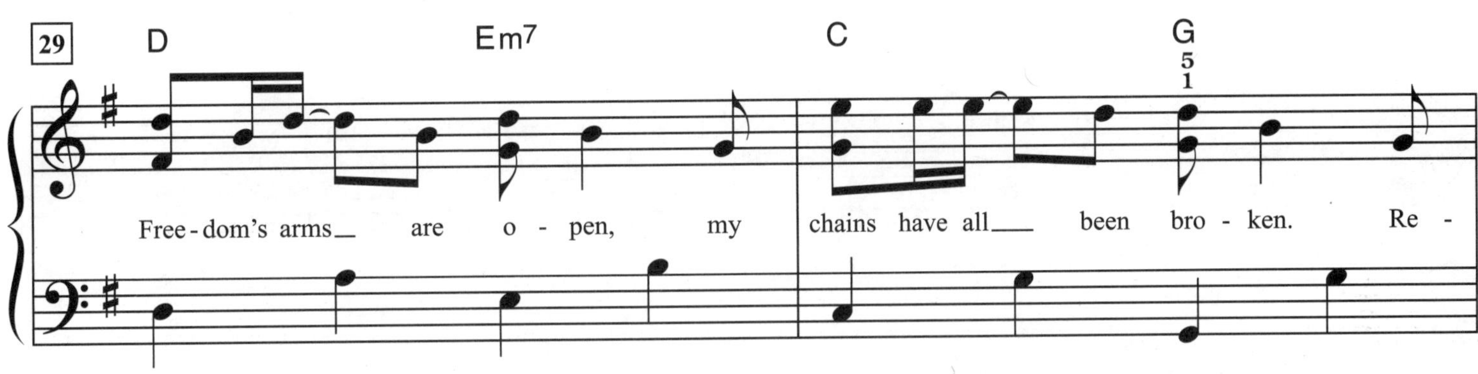
29
D
Em7
C
G
Free-dom's arms are o - pen, my
chains have all been bro - ken. Re -

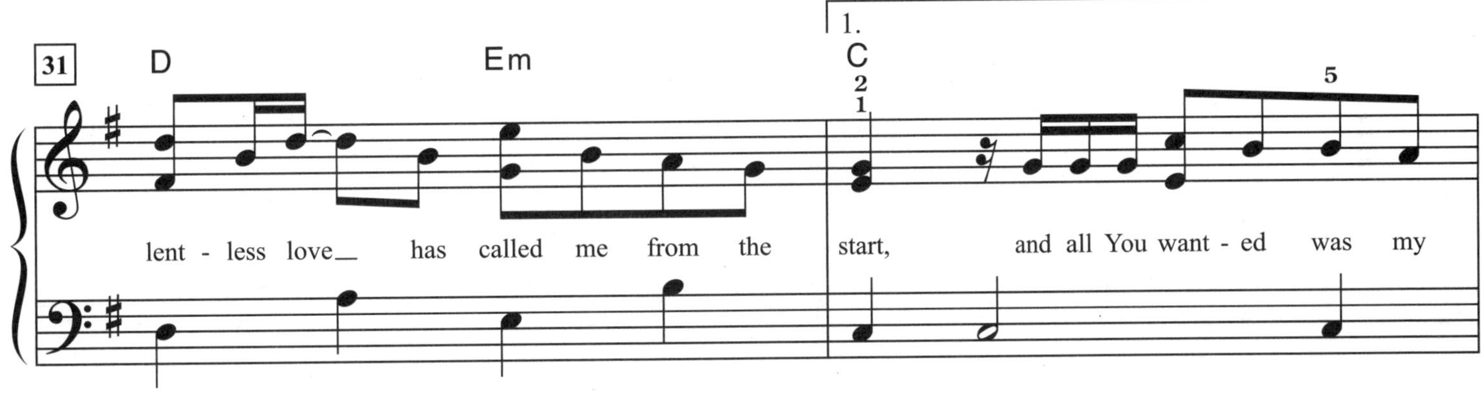
31
D
Em
1.
C
lent - less love has called me from the
start, and all You want - ed was my

33
D
Em
C
G
heart.
3. I was

2.
35
C
Am7
Em
to Coda
start, all You want - ed was my heart.
Bridge:
37
D
Am
Em
No more chains, I've been set free.
39
D
Am
Em
No more fight - ing bat - tles that You've won for me. Oh,
41
D
Am
Em7
D
D.S. al Coda
now in Christ I stand com - plete!
Coda
C
D
Em7
All You've want - ed was my heart.

Verse 3:
I was chasing healing when I'd been made well,
I was fighting battles when You conquered hell.
Living free but from a prison cell;
Lord, I lay it down today.

So I'll stop living off of how I feel,
And start standing on Your truth revealed.
Jesus is my strength, my shield,
And He will never fail me.

BEAUTIFUL DAY

Words and Music by Chris Stevens,
Jamie Grace, Morgan Harper Nichols
and Toby McKeehan
Arr. Carol Tornquist

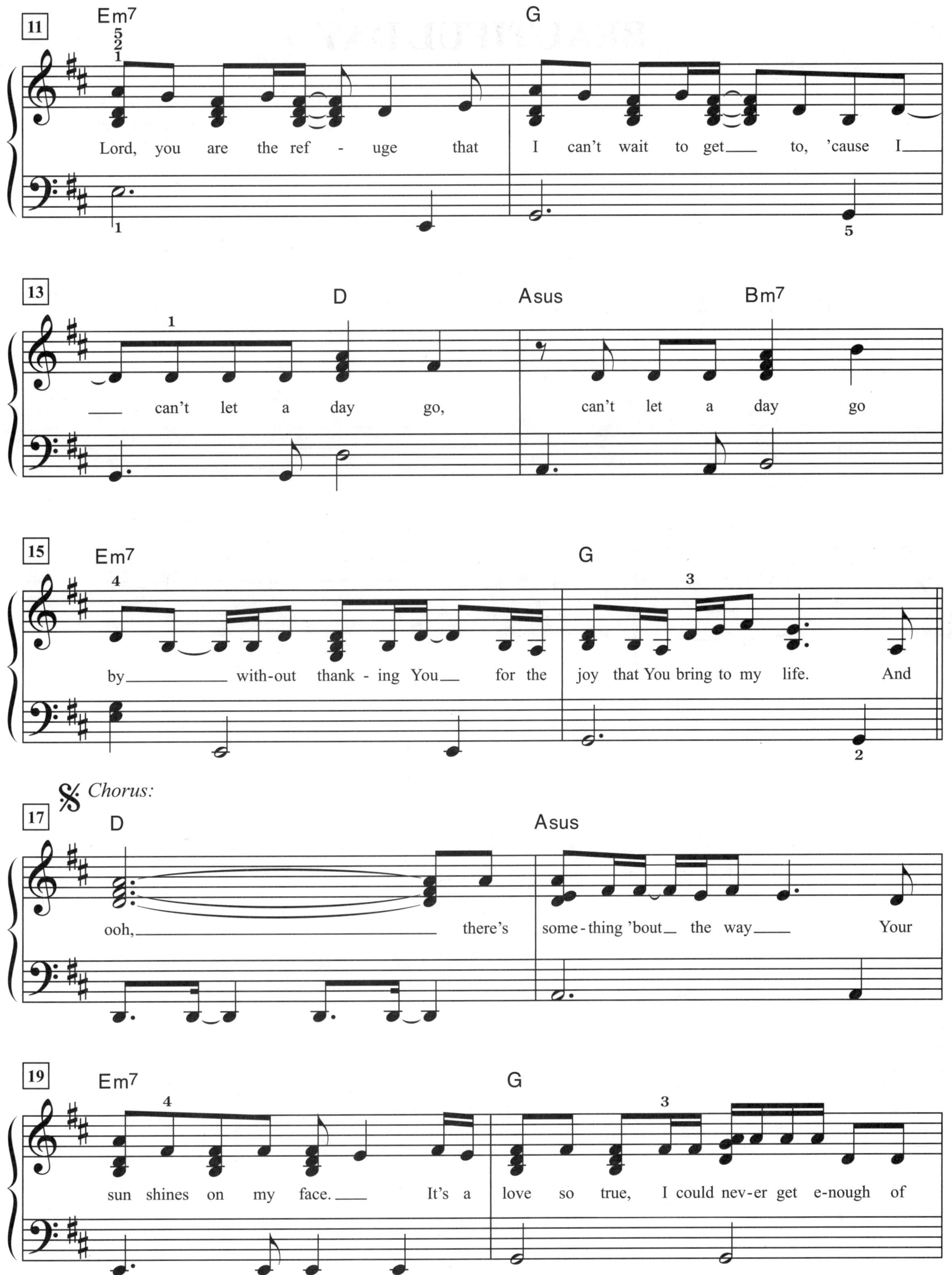
11
Em7
G
Lord, you are the ref - uge that I can't wait to get to, 'cause I
13
D
Asus
Bm7
can't let a day go, can't let a day go
15
Em7
G
by with-out thank - ing You for the joy that You bring to my life. And
Chorus:
17
D
Asus
ooh, there's some-thing 'bout the way Your
19
Em7
G
sun shines on my face. It's a love so true, I could nev-er get e-nough of

21
D
A
You. This feel - ing can't be wrong. I'm a - bout to
23
Em7
G
get my wor - ship on. Take me a - way, it's a beau - ti - ful day!
25
D
A
Yeah, it's a beau - ti ful day!
27
Em7
to Coda
1.
G
Yeah!
2.
Bridge:
29
G
G
I've got no need to wor - ry, I've

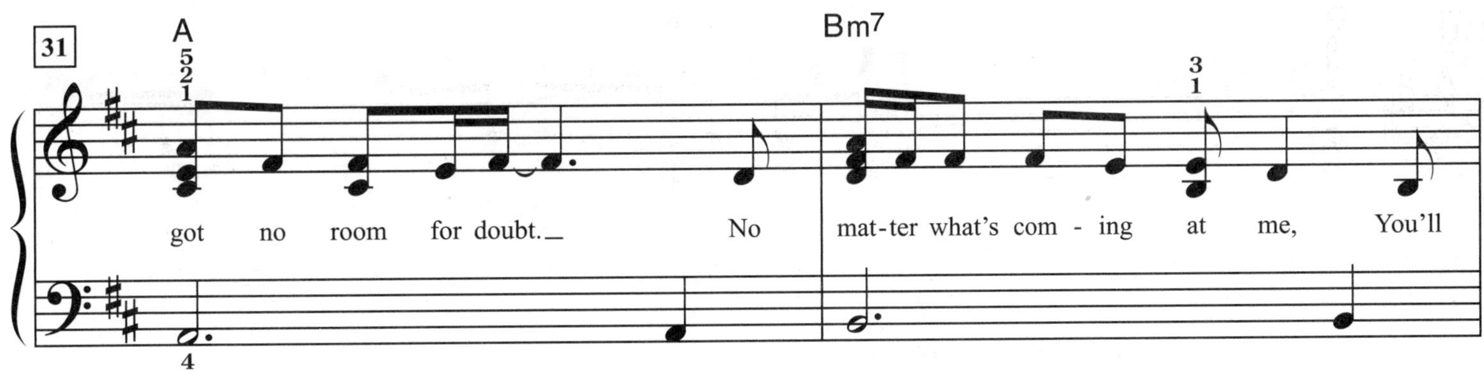

Verse 2:
When trouble seems to rain on my dreams, it's not a big, not a big deal.
Let it wash all the bugs off my windshield, 'cause You're showing me in You, I'm free.
And You're still the refuge that I've just gotta get to.
So, I won't let a day go, won't let a day go by.
So put the drop top down, turn it up, I'm ready to fly.

FOREVER

Words and Music by Brian Johnson,
Christa Black Gifford, Gabe Wilson,
Jenn Johnson, Joel Taylor and Kari Jobe
Arr. Carol Tornquist

Worshipful ballad

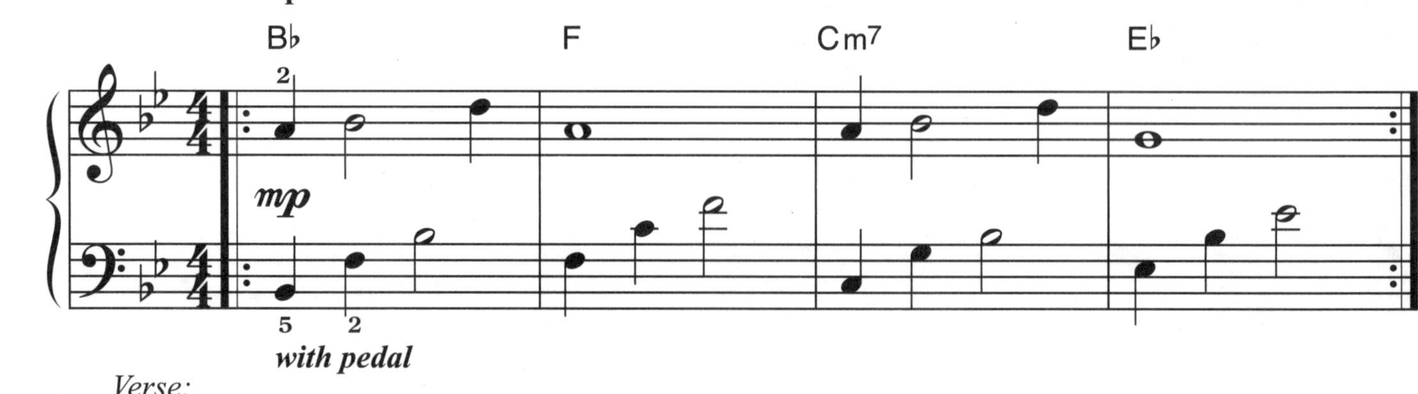

Verse:

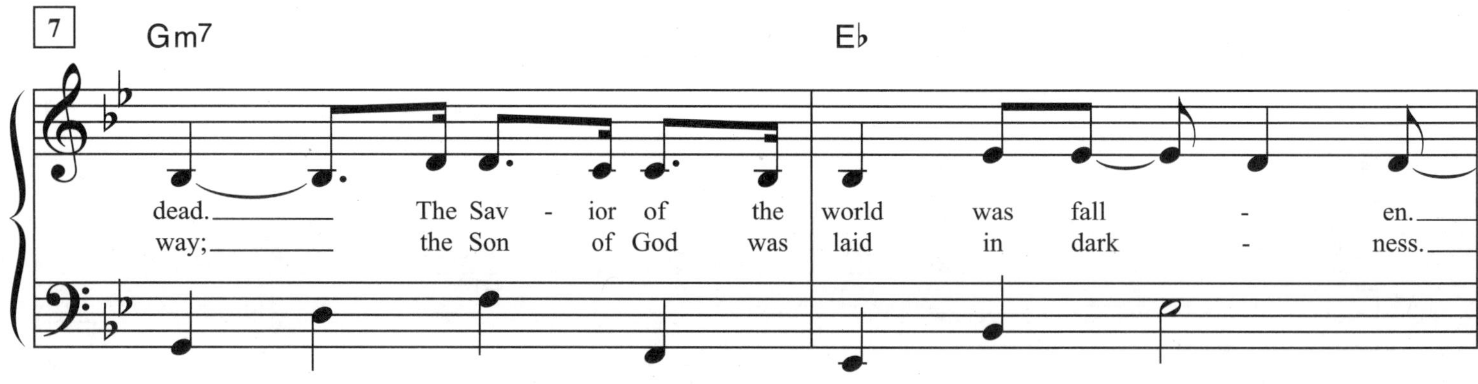

11
Gm7
1.
E♭
B♭
us, the weight of ev - 'ry curse up - on Him.
waged, the pow'r of hell for-
14
F
Cm7
E♭
2.
Pre-Chorus:
17
E♭
B♭
F
ev - er bro - ken. The ground be-gan to shake, the stone was rolled a-
20
Gm
E♭
B♭
way. His per - fect love could not be o - ver - come. Now death, where is your
23
F
Gm
E♭
sting? Our res - ur-rect - ed King has ren-dered you de - feat - ed. For -

Chorus:
26
B♭sus B♭ F Gm7
mf
ev - er He is glo - ri - fied. For - ev - er He is
29
E♭ B♭sus B♭ F
lift - ed high. For - ev - er He is ris - en. He is a - live!
32
G
1.
E♭
He is a - live!
34
2.
E♭ B♭ F
For - ev - er!
37
Gm7 E♭ B♭

40
F
Gm7
E♭
43
B♭
F
Cm7
Bridge:
46
E♭
B♭
F
We sing hal - le - lu - jah! We sing hal - le - lu -
49
Gm
E♭
B♭
jah! We sing hal - le - lu - jah! The Lamb has o - ver - come. We sing hal - le - lu -
52
F
Gm
E♭
jah! We sing hal - le - lu - jah! We sing hal - le - lu - jah! The Lamb has o - ver -

55
B♭
F
Gm
come. We sing hal - le - lu - jah! We sing hal - le - lu - jah! We sing hal - le - lu -
58
E♭
B♭
F
jah! The Lamb has o - ver - come. We sing hal - le - lu jah! We sing hal - le - lu -
61
Gm
E♭
B♭
jah! We sing hal - le - lu - jah! The Lamb has o - ver - come. We sing hal - le-lu -
64
F
Gm
E♭
jah! We sing hal - le-lu - jah! We sing hal - le-lu - jah! The Lamb has o - ver -
67
B♭
F
Gm
come! We sing hal - le-lu - jah! We sing hal - le-lu - jah! We sing hal - le-lu -

Chorus:

70
E♭
B♭sus
B♭
jah! The Lamb has o - ver - come. For - ev - er He is
f

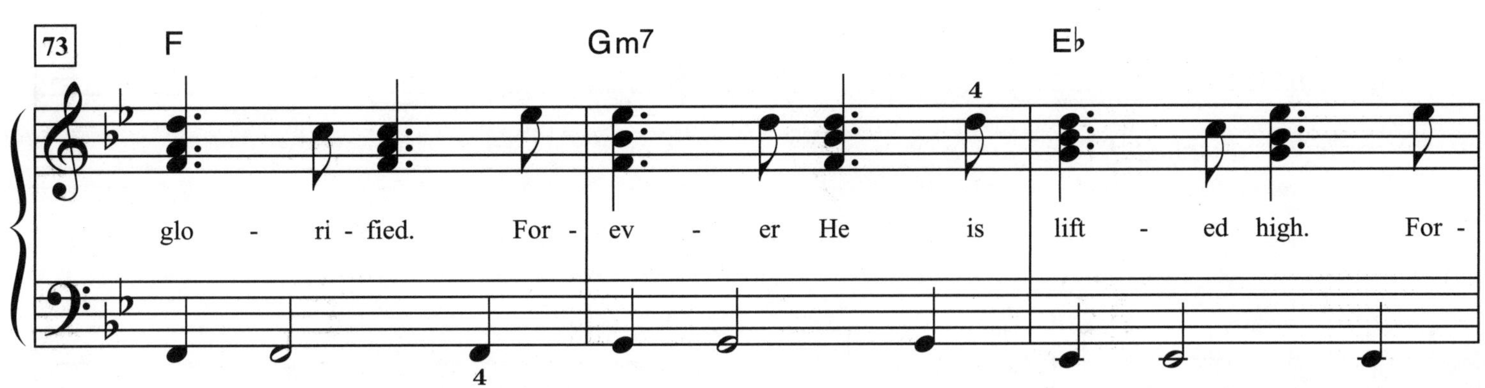
73
F
Gm7
E♭
glo - ri - fied. For - ev - er He is lift - ed high. For -

76
B♭sus
B♭
F
Gm7
E♭
ev - er He is ris - en. He is a - live! He is a - live!

79
1.
2.
E♭
B♭
For -
molto rit.

I AM

Words and Music by
David Crowder and Ed Cash
Arr. Carol Tornquist

17
C
Verse:
I am hold - ing on, I am.
3. Love like this, O my
21
Am7
Gsus
God, to find! I am o - ver-whelmed with a joy di - vine! Love like this sets our
25
Chorus:
C
hearts on fire!
mf
I am hold-ing on to You. I
29
Am7
F
am hold-ing on to You. In the mid-dle of the storm, I am hold - ing on to You.
33
C
1.
2.
I

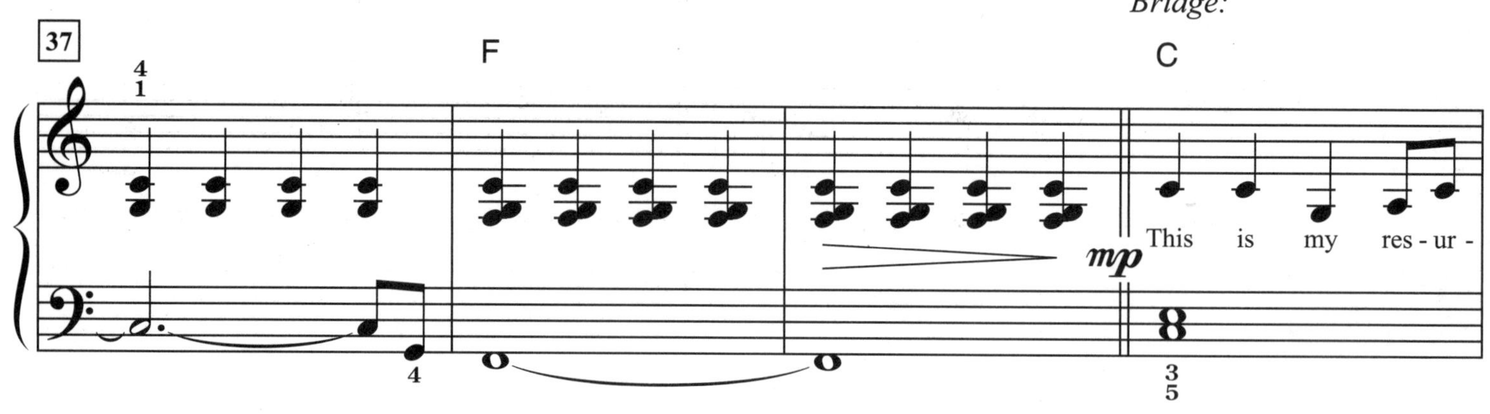
Bridge:
37
F
C
mp
This is my res - ur -

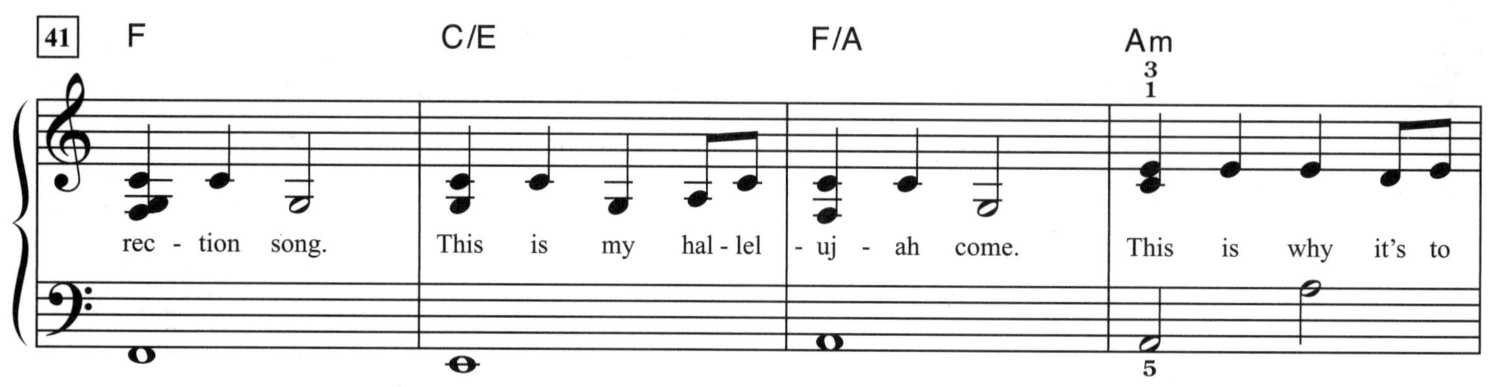
41
F
C/E
F/A
Am
rec - tion song.
This is my hal - lel
- uj - ah come.
This is why it's to

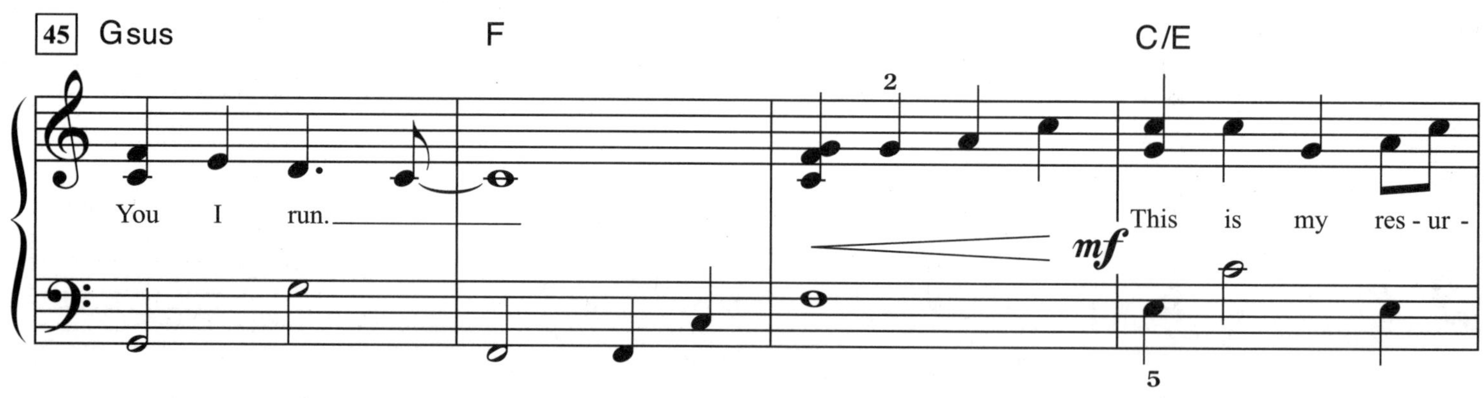
45
Gsus
F
C/E
You I run.
mf
This is my res - ur -

49
F
C/E
F
Am7
rec - tion song.
This is my hal - le -
lu - jah come.
This is why it's to

53
Gsus
C/E
F
C/G
You I run.
There's no space that His
love can't reach,
there's no place where we

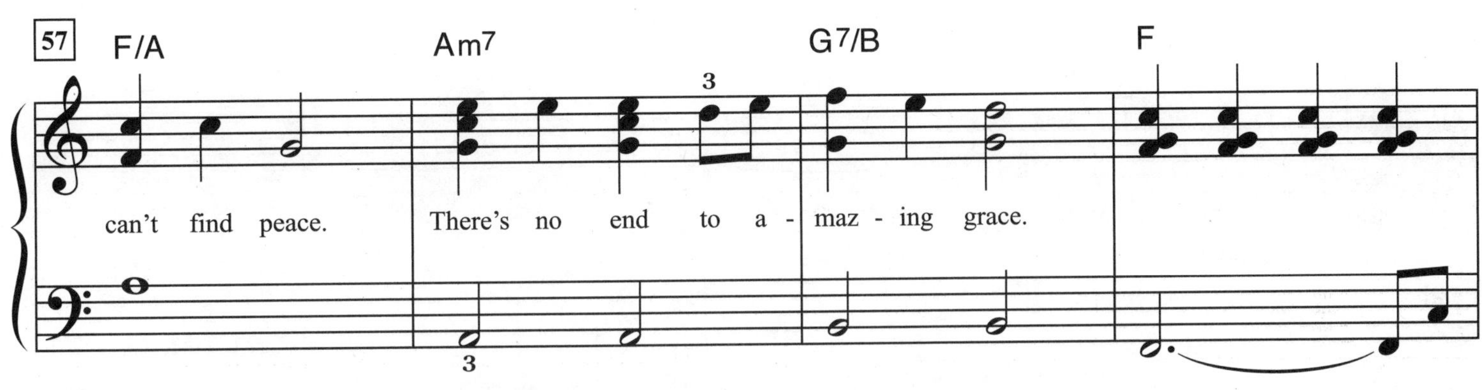
57
F/A
Am7
G7/B
F
can't find peace.
There's no end to a - maz - ing grace.

Chorus:
61
C
Am7
f
I am hold-ing on to You. I am hold-ing

65
F
C
on to You. In the mid-dle of the storm,
I am hold - ing on. I
am hold-ing

69
Am7
F
on to You. I am holding on to You. In the middle of the storm,

73
C
Am7
I am hold - ing on to You.

77
F
In the mid - dle of the storm,
mf

79
C
I am hold - ing on to You.
rit.
mp

LORD, I NEED YOU

Words and Music by Christy Nockels,
Daniel Carson, Jesse Reeves,
Kristian Stanfill and Matt Maher
Arr. Carol Tornquist

LORD, I NEED YOU

Words and Music by Christy Nockels,
Daniel Carson, Jesse Reeves,
Kristian Stanfill and Matt Maher
Arr. Carol Tornquist

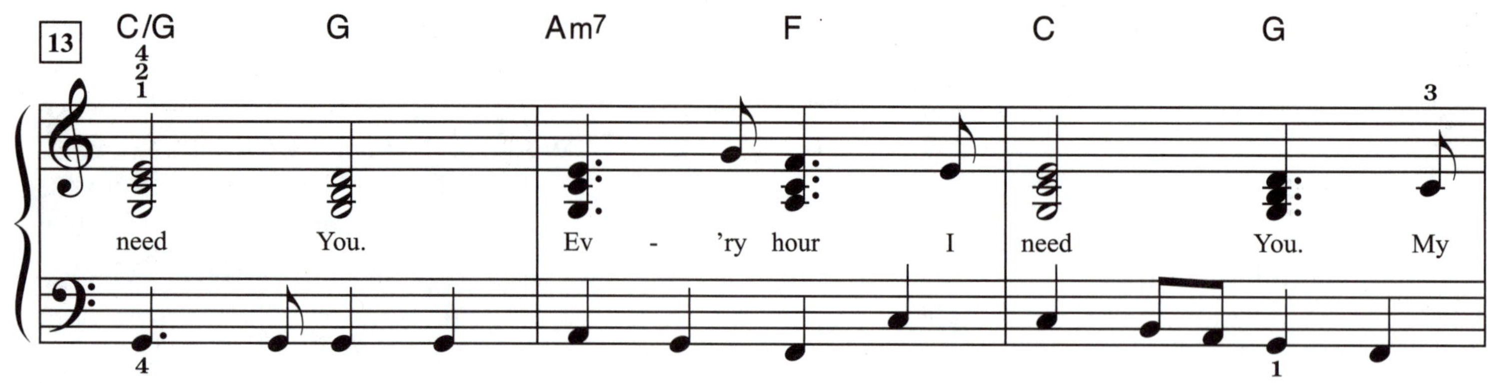
13
C/G G Am7 F C G
need You. Ev - 'ry hour I need You. My

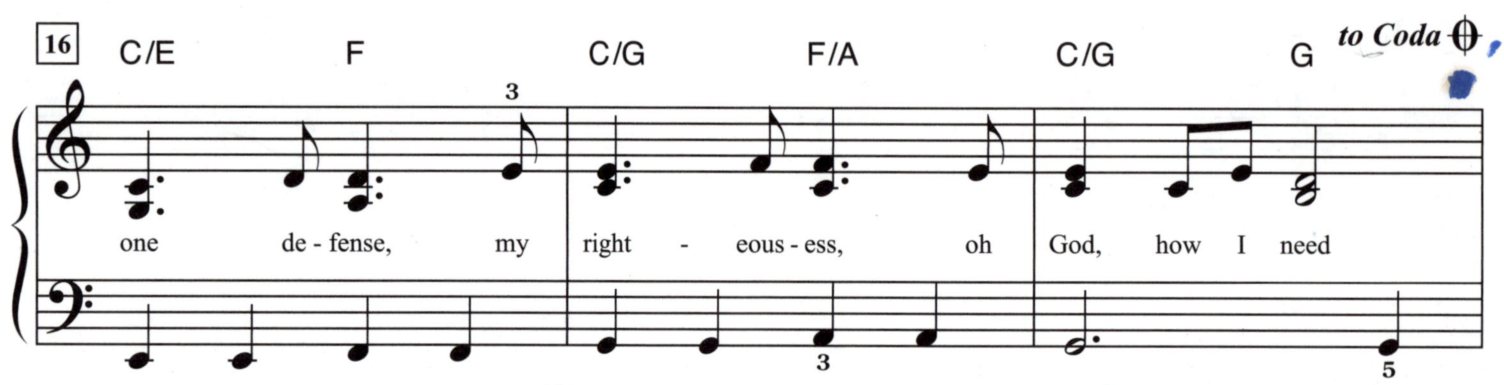
16
C/E F C/G F/A C/G G
to Coda
one de - fense, my right - eous - ess, oh God, how I need

19
1.
C F/C
You. 2. Where sin runs
2.
C
You. So

Bridge:

22
F C/E G/B Am7 F G
teach my song to rise to You when temp - ta - tions come my

25
F
C/E
G/B
Am7
way.
and
When I
can - not stand, I'll fall on
You.
28
F
G
C
F/C
D.S. al Coda
Je - sus, You're my hope and
stay.
Lord, I
chorus
Coda
C
C/E
F
C/G
F/A
You.
You're my
one de - fense, my
right - eous - ness. Oh
34
C/G
G
C
C/E
F
God, how I need
You.
My
one de - fense, my
37
C/G
F/A
C/G
G7sus
C
right - eous - ness, Oh
rit.
God, how I need
You.
mp

OCEANS (WHERE FEET MAY FAIL)

Words and Music by Joel Houston,
Matt Crocker and Salomon Ligthelm
Arr. Carol Tornquist

14
A
G
D
A
Your name
and keep my eyes a-bove
the waves.
When o - ceans

17
G
D
A
1.
G
A
rise, my soul will rest in Your
em-brace, for I am
Yours
and You are

20
Bm7
A/C♯
D
A
G
mine.

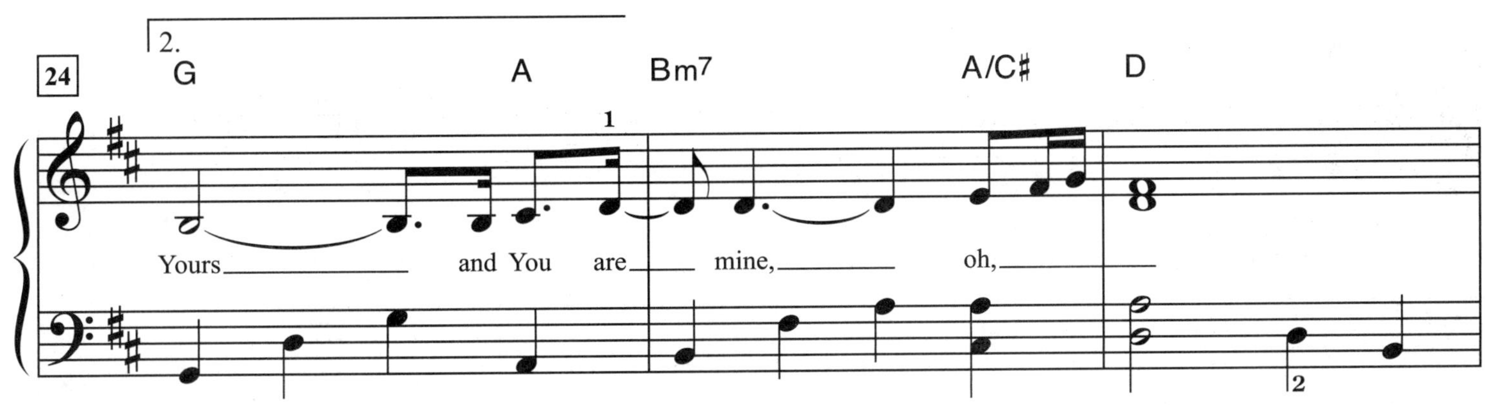
2.
24
G
A
Bm7
A/C♯
D
Yours
and You are
mine,
oh,

27
A
G
Bm7
A/C♯
And You are mine, oh.
30
D
A
G
Bridge:
33
Bm
G
D
A
37
Bm
G
D
mf
Spir-it, lead me where my trust is with - out bor-ders. Let me walk up-on the wa-ters wher-
40
A
Bm
G
ev - er You would call me.
Take me deep-er than my feet could ev - er wan-der, and my

43
D
A
faith will be made strong - er in the pres - ence of my Sav - ior.
Chorus:
45
G D A G D
I will call up-on Your name and keep my eyes a-bove
48
A G D A
the waves. When o - ceans rise, my soul will rest in Your em-brace, for I am
51
G A Bm7 A/C♯ D A
Yours and You are mine.
rit. e dim.
55
Em Bm7 D
p

THE ONLY NAME (YOURS WILL BE)

Words and Music by Benji Cowart
Arr. Carol Tornquist

13
2., 3.
F
G
mf
And Yours is the name, the name that has saved me,
16
C
Am7
F
mer - cy and grace, the pow'r that for - gave me and Your love is all
19
G
C
3.
Csus
D.S.
I've ev - er need - ed.
Yours will be
4.
Chorus:
22
F/C
C
When I wake up in the Land of Glo - ry and
25
F
Dm7
with the saints, I will tell my sto - ry, there will be one

28
G/B
C
1.
Csus
2.
Csus
name that I pro - claim.
When
32
C
F
Je - sus,
Je - sus,
36
Dm7
G/B
C
Csus
Je - sus, just that name.
Bridge:
40
C
F
La la la la la la la la la la
la la la la la la la la la la
44
Dm7
G/B
C
la la la la la la la la la la la la
la.
rit.

SPEAK LIFE

Words and Music by Jamie Moore,
Ryan Stevenson and Toby McKeehan
Arr. Carol Tornquist

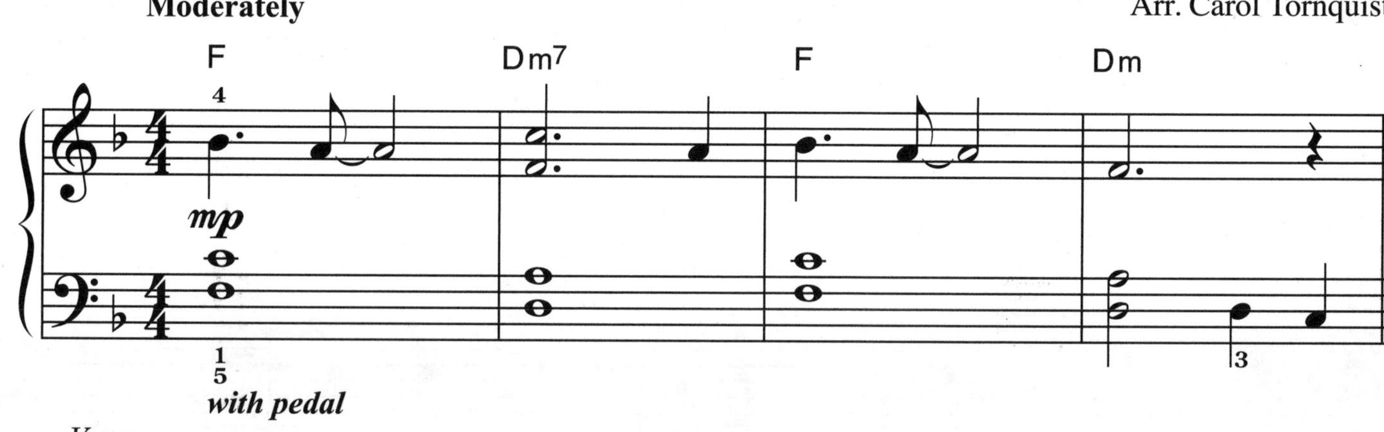

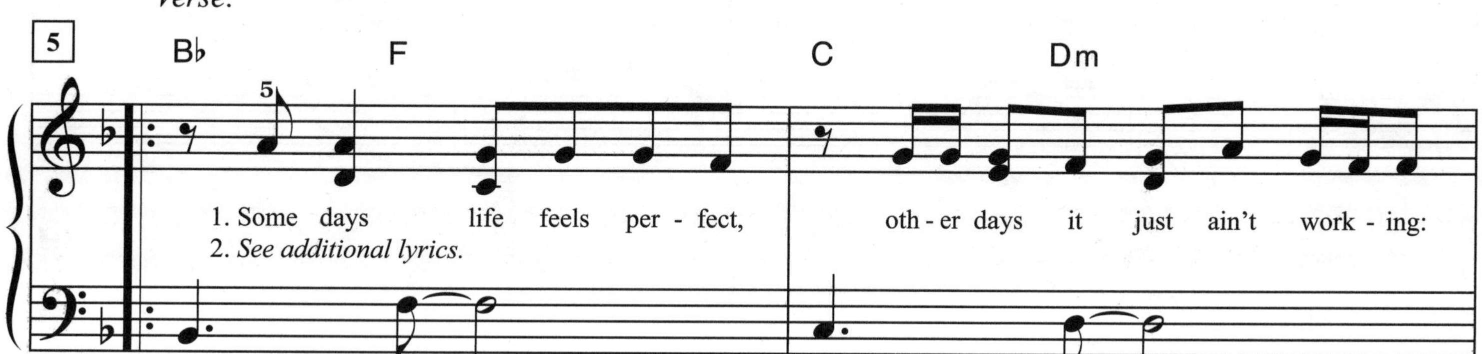

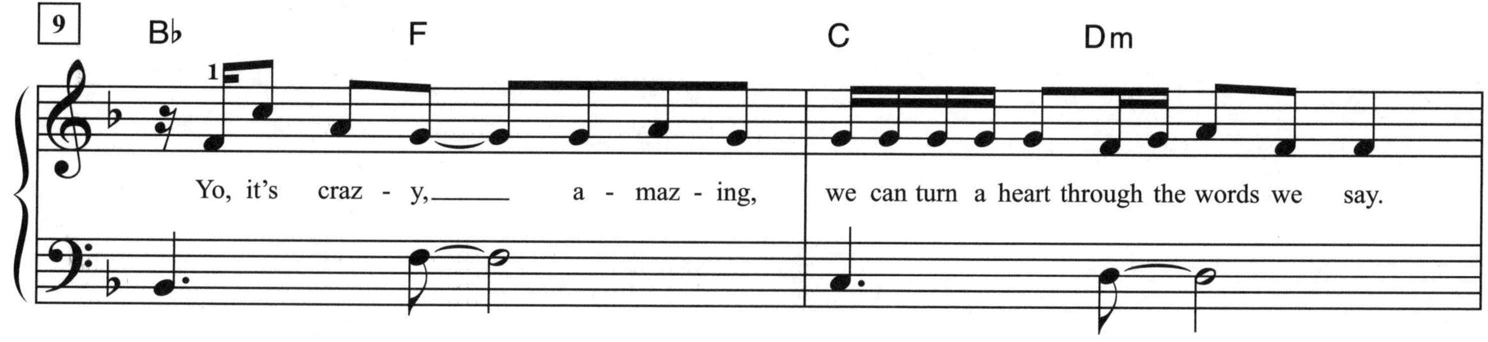

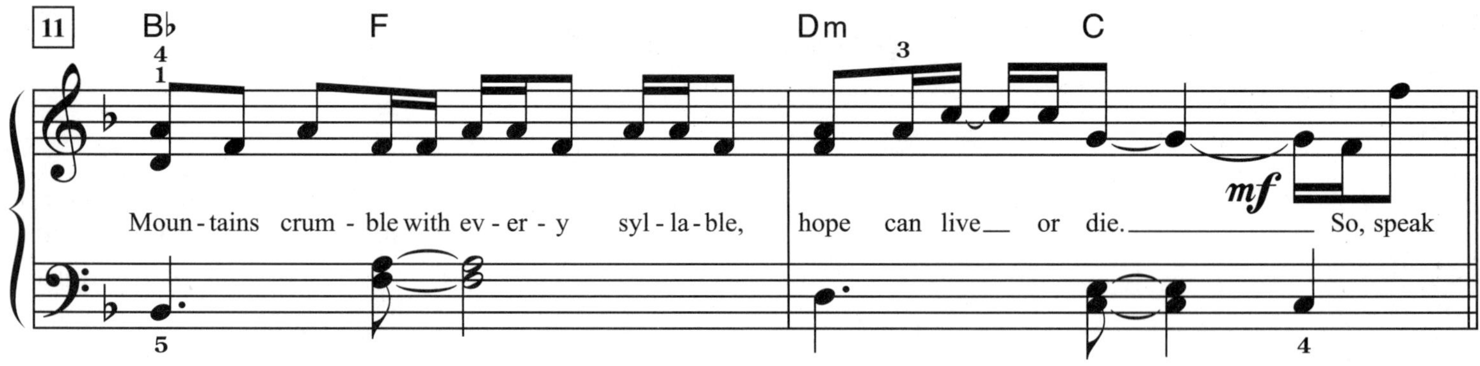
11
B♭
F
Dm
C
Moun - tains crum - ble with ev - er - y syl - la - ble,
hope can live or die.
mf
So, speak

Chorus:

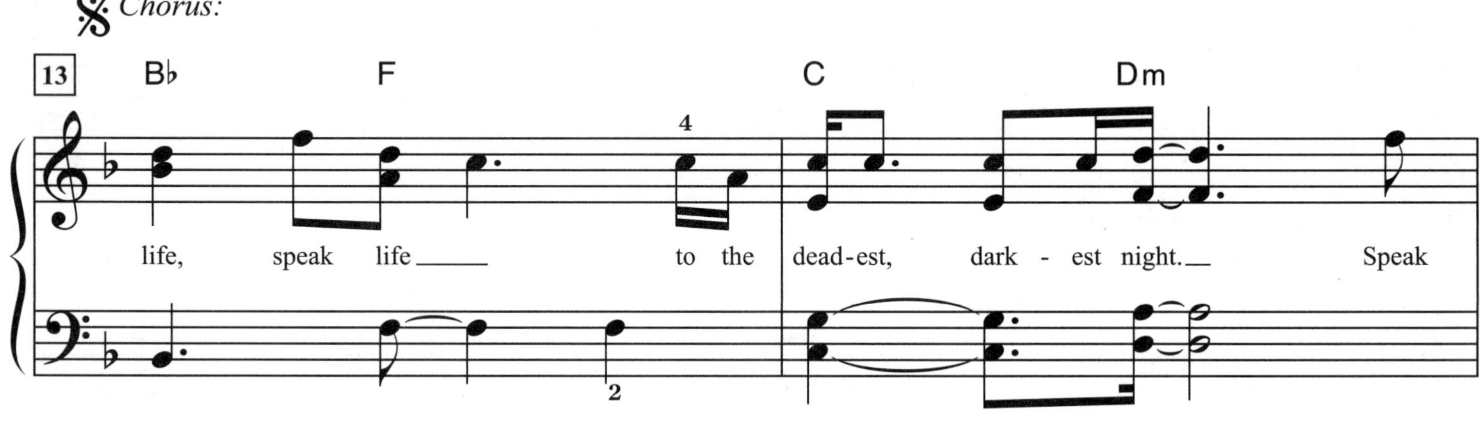
13
B♭
F
C
Dm
life, speak life to the dead - est, dark - est night.
Speak

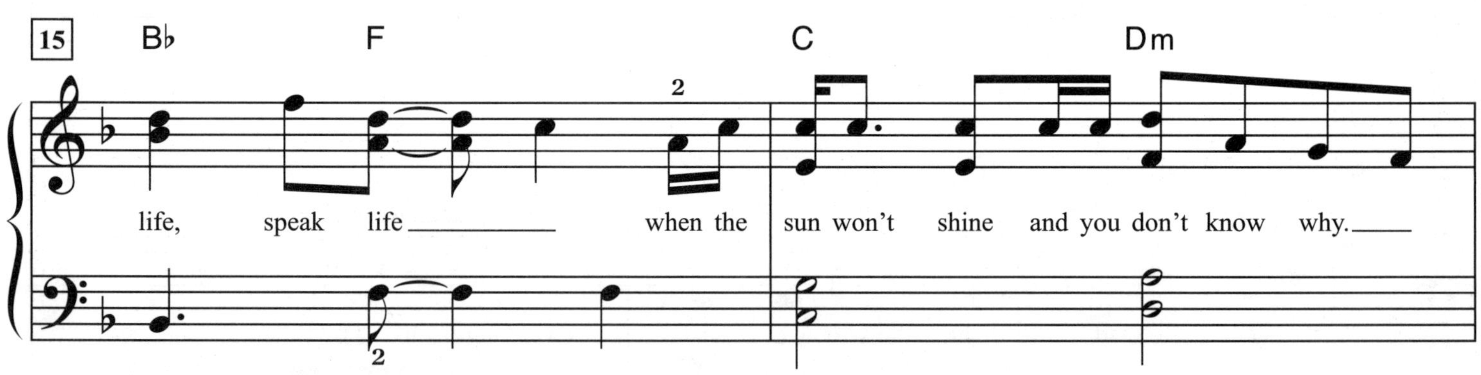
15
B♭
F
C
Dm
life, speak life when the sun won't shine and you don't know why.

17
B♭
F
C
Dm7
Look in - to the eyes of the bro - ken - heart - ed.
Watch them come a - live as soon as you speak

19
B♭
F
C
1
2
3
5
hope, you speak love, you speak, you speak

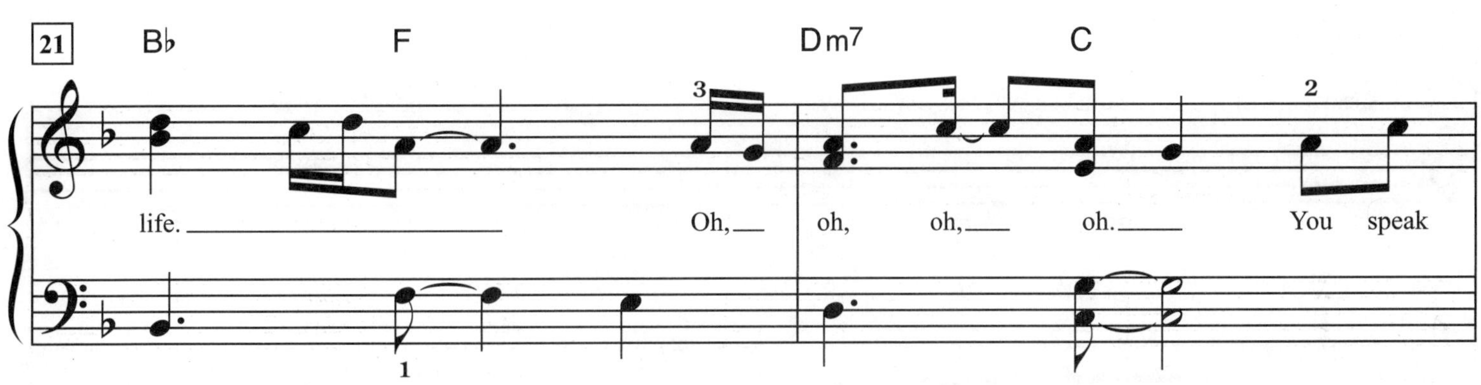
21
B♭
F
Dm7
C
3
2
1
life. Oh, oh, oh, oh. You speak

to Coda
1.
23
B♭
F
Dm7
C
life. Oh, oh, oh, oh.

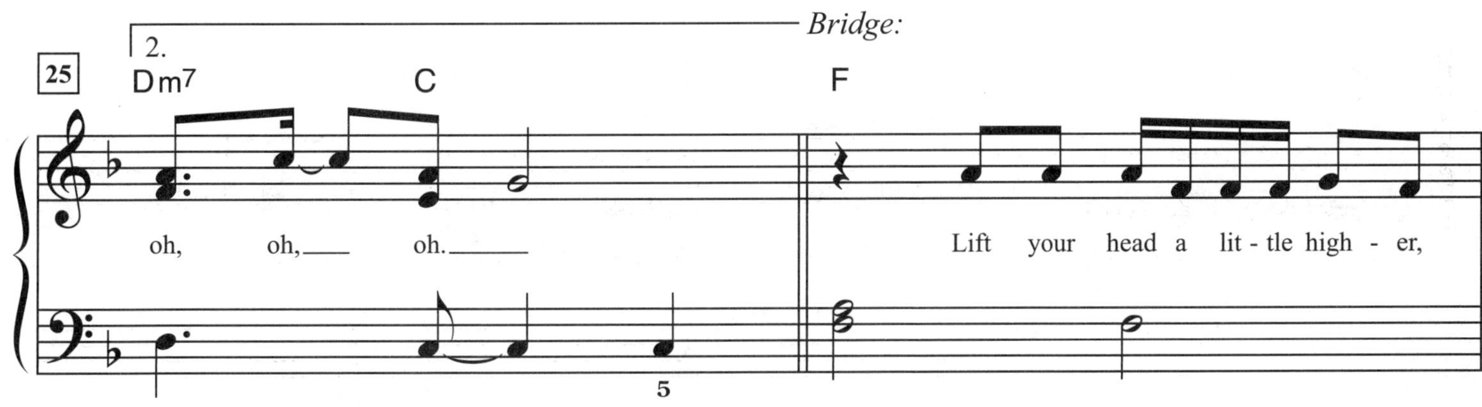
2.
Bridge:
25
Dm7
C
F
5
oh, oh, oh.
Lift your head a lit - tle high - er,

27
Dm
F
spread the love like fi - re.
Hope will fall like rain when you
29
B♭
F
speak life with the words you say.
Raise your thoughts a lit - tle high - er,
31
Dm7
F/C
use your words to in - spire.
Joy will fall like rain when you
33
B♭
F
speak life with the things you say.
Lift your head a lit - tle high - er,
35
Dm7
F
spread the love like fi - re.
Hope will fall like rain when you

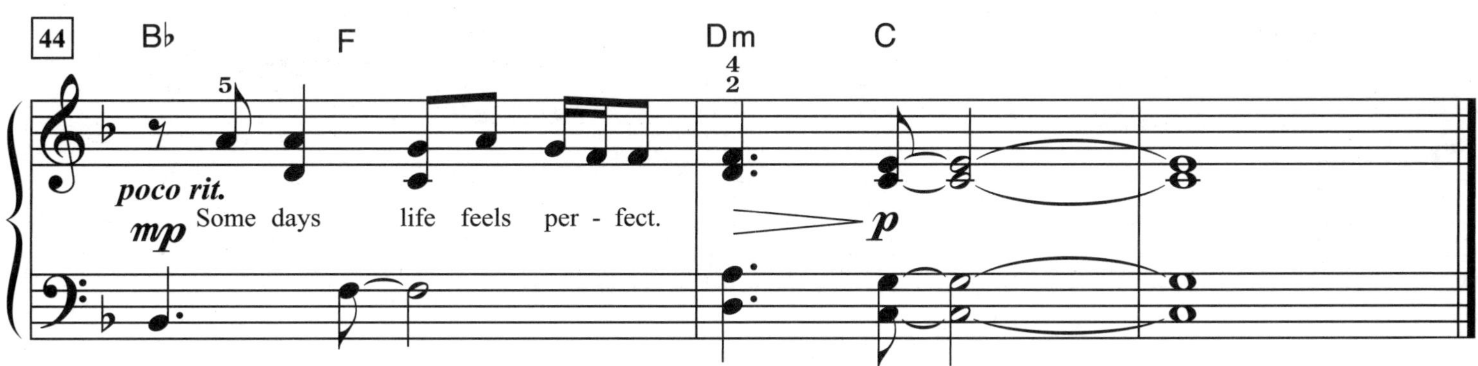

Verse 2:
Some days the tongue gets twisted,
Other days my thoughts just fall apart.
I do, I don't, I will, I won't.
It's like I'm drowning in the deep.
Well, it's crazy to imagine words from our lips
As the arms of compassion.
Mountains crumble with every syllable.
Hope can live or die.

OVERCOMER

Words and Music by Ben Glover,
Chris Stevens and David Garcia
Arr. Carol Tornquist

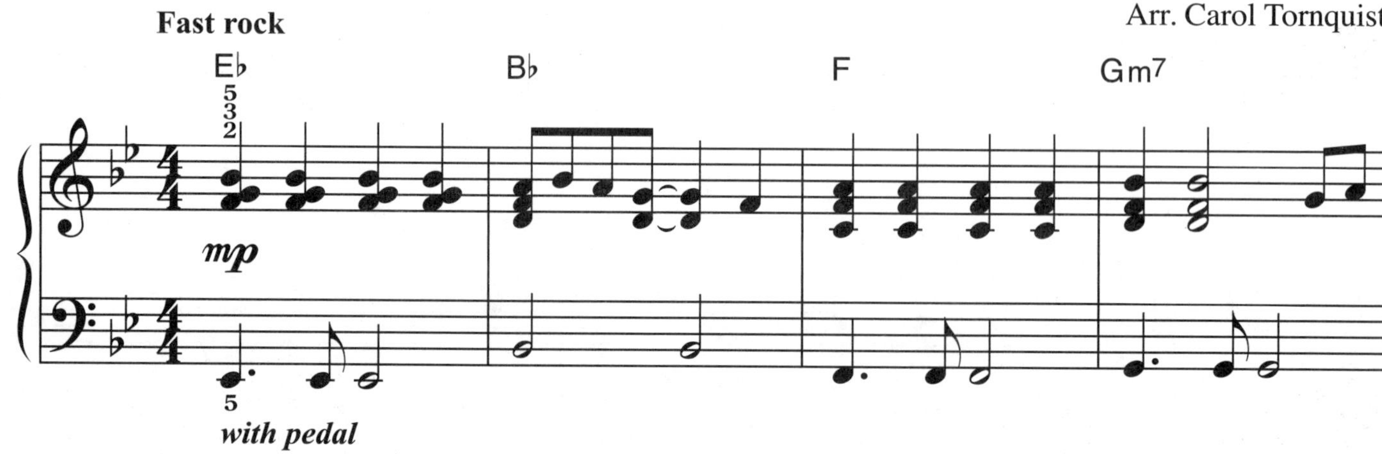

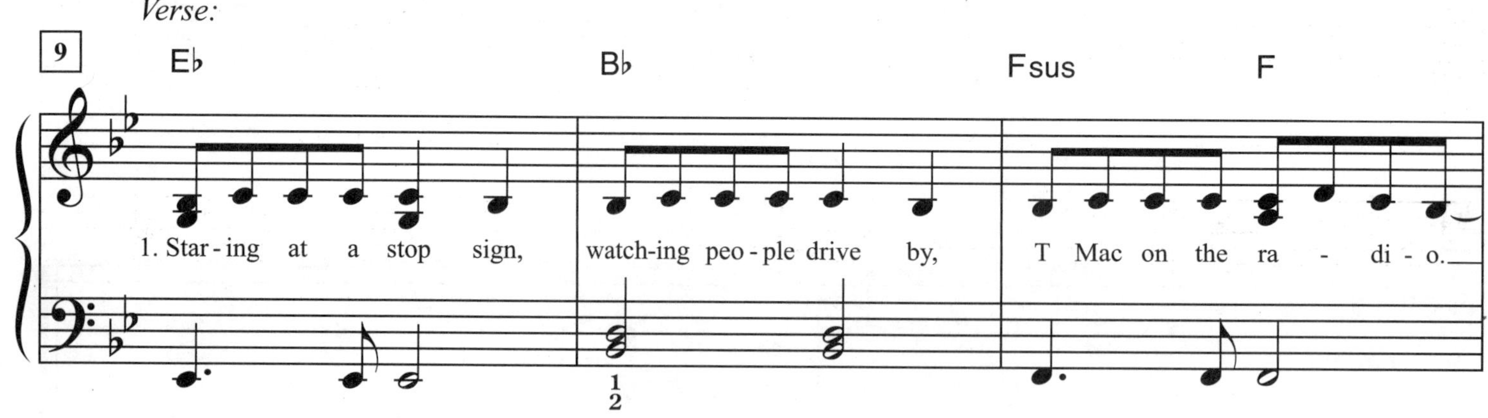

15
Fsus
F
Gm
E♭
look - ing for a ray of hope.
Ooh

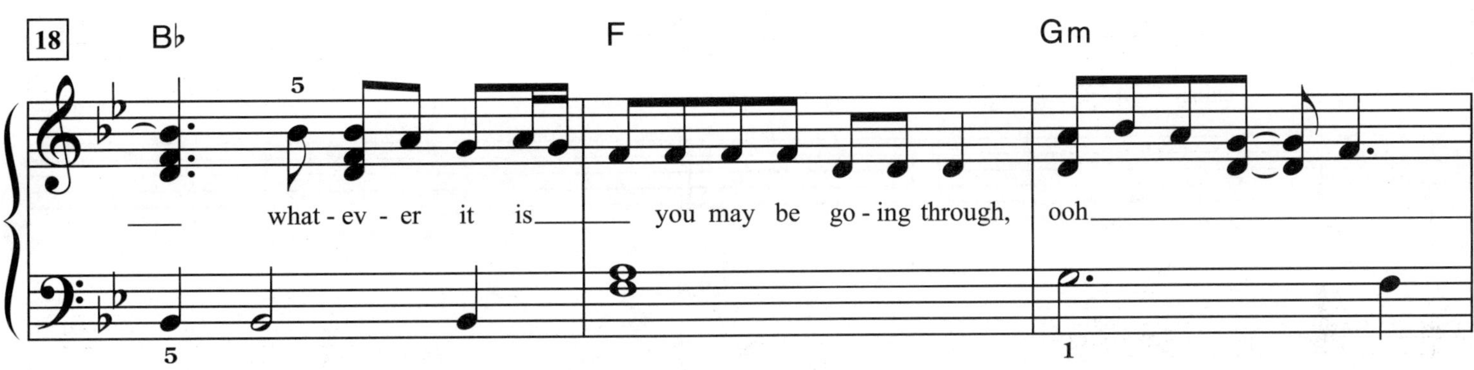
18
B♭
F
Gm
what - ev - er it is
you may be go - ing through,
ooh

21
E♭
B♭
F
I know He's not gon - na let
it get the best of you.

Chorus:
24
E♭
B♭
You're an o - ver - com -
er!
Stay in the fight
mf

27
F
Gm7
E♭
till the fi - nal round. You're not go - ing un - der,
30
B♭
F
Gm7
'cause God is hold - ing you right now. You might be down
33
E♭
B♭
Dm7
for a mo-ment, feel - ing like it's hope-less. That's when He re-minds you
36
Gm7
E♭
B♭
that you're an o - ver-com - er! You're an o - ver-com -
39
Dm7
to Coda
Gm7
E♭
er!

Verse:

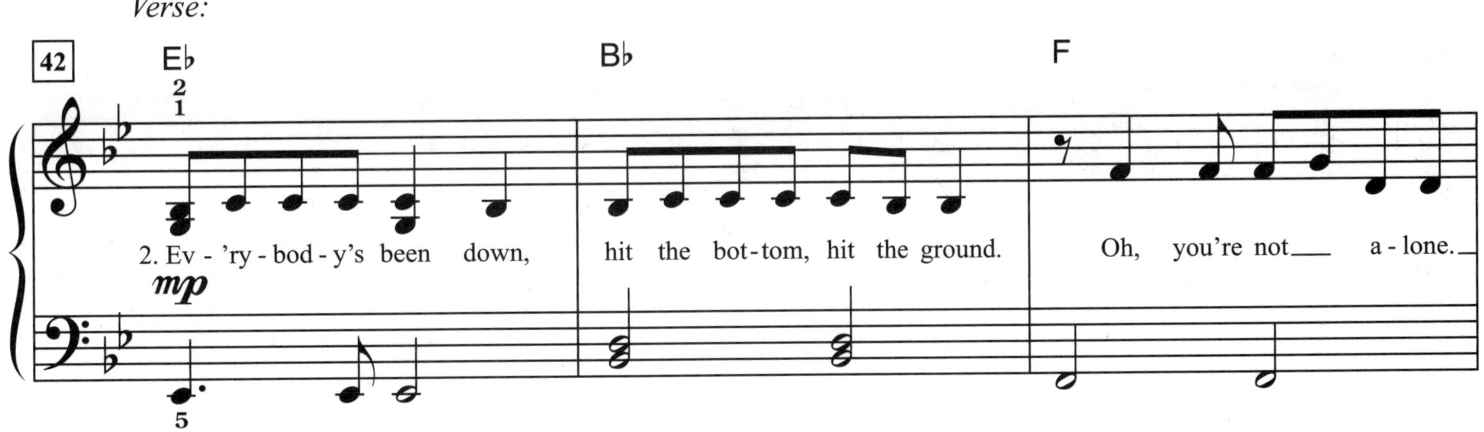

Chorus:

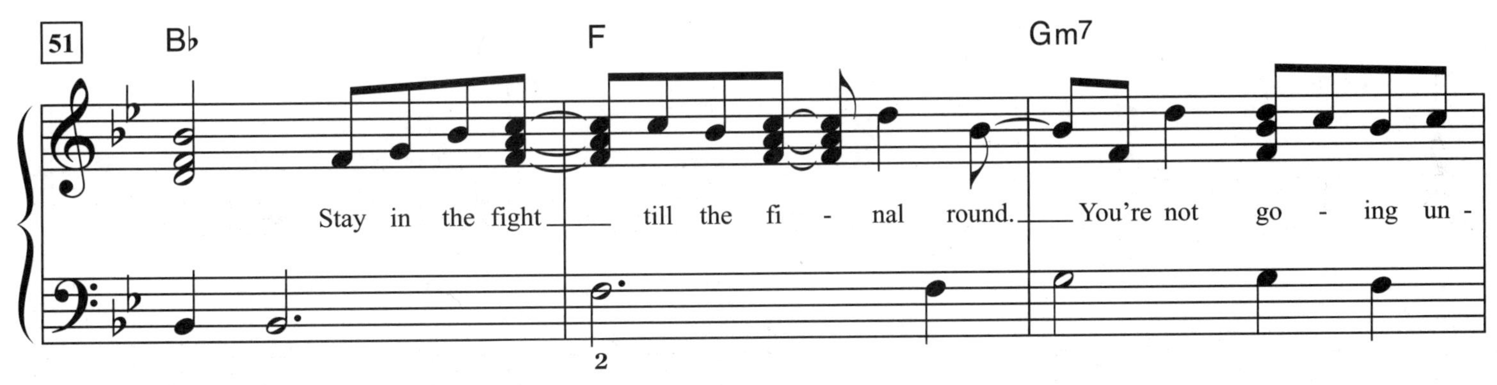

54
E♭
B♭
F
der,
'cause God is hold - ing you right now.

57
Gm7
E♭
B♭
You might be down for a mo-ment, feel - ing like it's hope-less. That's

60
Dm7
Gm7
E♭
when He re - minds you that you're an o - ver - com - er!

63
B♭
Dm7
Gm7
You're an o - ver - com - er! The

Bridge:
66
E♭
Cm7
Gm
same Man, the great I AM, the One who o - ver-came death is liv - ing in - side you!
69
B♭
F
E♭
Cm7
So, just hold tight, fix your eyes on the One who holds your life.
72
Gm
Fsus
F
E♭
There's noth - ing He can't do! He's tell - ing you
75
B♭
F
Gm7
D.S. al Coda
you're an o - ver - com -
Coda
Gm7
E♭
B♭
mp
rit.

SHAKE

Words and Music by Bart Millard,
Ben Glover, David Garcia and Solomon Olds
Arr. Carol Tornquist

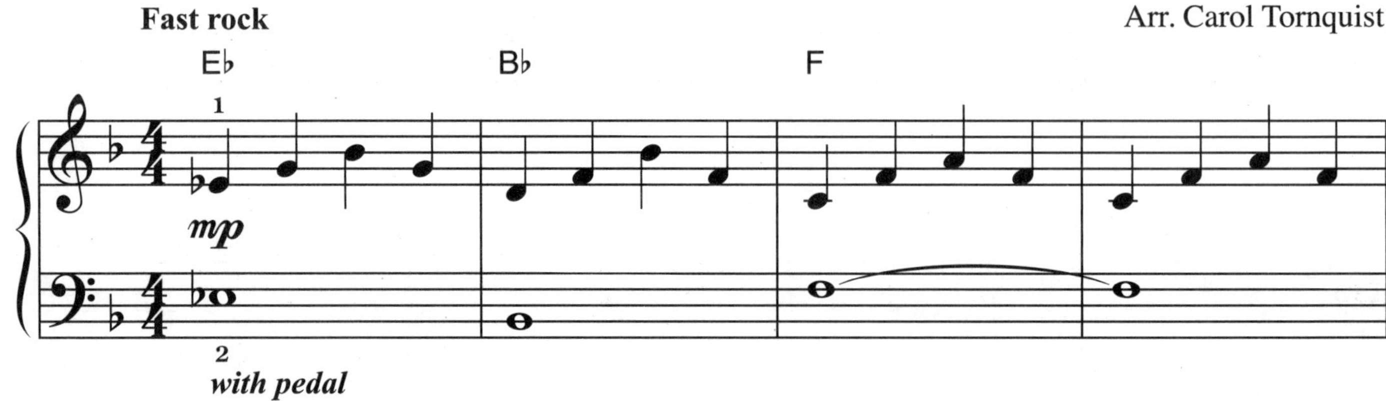

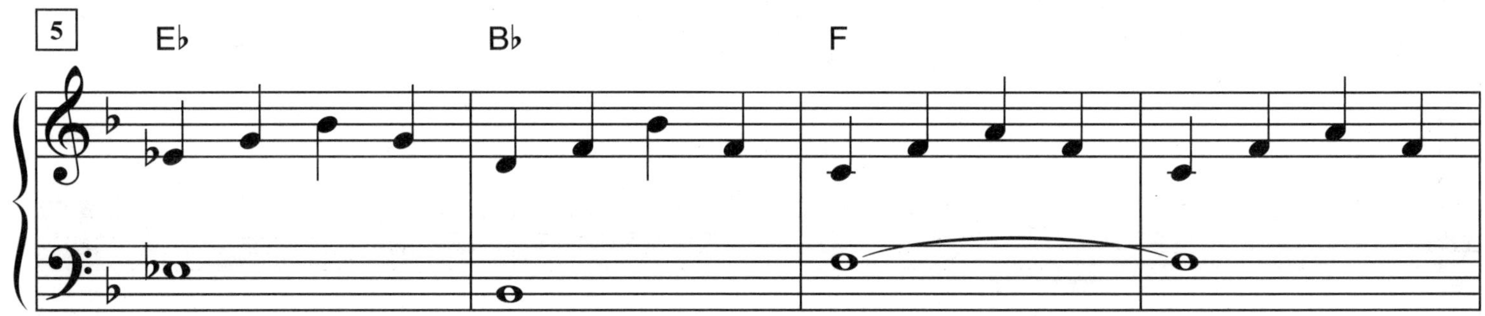

16
F7
B♭/F
F
All that I know is my heart was broke and I don't
19
F7
ever wan-na go back.
Verse:
F
1. Ain't no ex - pla - na -
2. See additional lyrics.
22
F7
tion how I saw the light. He
25
found me and He set me free, and He brought me back to life.
28
F7sus
Blame it on the trans - for - ma - tion, changed

31
F7
Bb7/F
Fm
down to the core.
His love is real and I can't
34
Bb7/F
F
Bb7/F
F7
F7sus
F
sit still, 'cause my name's not shamed no more, more, more. Great
37
Bb7
F
God Al-might-y done changed me. Great God Al-might-y, He done
Chorus:
40
Fm
Bb
Cm7
Bb
changed me. You got-ta shake, shake, shake like you're
43
Fm
Bb
Cm7
Bb
Fm
Bb7
changed, changed, changed. Brand new looks so

46
Cm7
B♭
Fm7
B♭
Cm7
B♭
good on you, so shake like you've been changed. Come on and
49
F
B♭
F
shake, shake like you've changed. Shake, shake
52
1.
2.
Chorus:
B♭
F
B♭
F
Fm
B♭
like you've changed. like you've changed, You got-ta shake, shake, shake
55
Cm7
B♭
Fm
B♭
Cm7
B♭
like you've changed, changed, changed.
58
Fm
B♭7
Cm7
B♭
Fm
B♭
Brand new looks so good on you, so shake like you've been changed.

61
Cm7
B♭
F
B♭
F
Come on and shake, shake like you've changed.
64
B♭
F
B♭/F
Shake, shake like you've changed.
67
F
B♭/F
F
Great
Bridge:
70
B♭7
Fm
God Al-might-y done changed me. Great God Al-might-y He done
73
B♭7
changed me. Great God Al-might-y He done me. Great

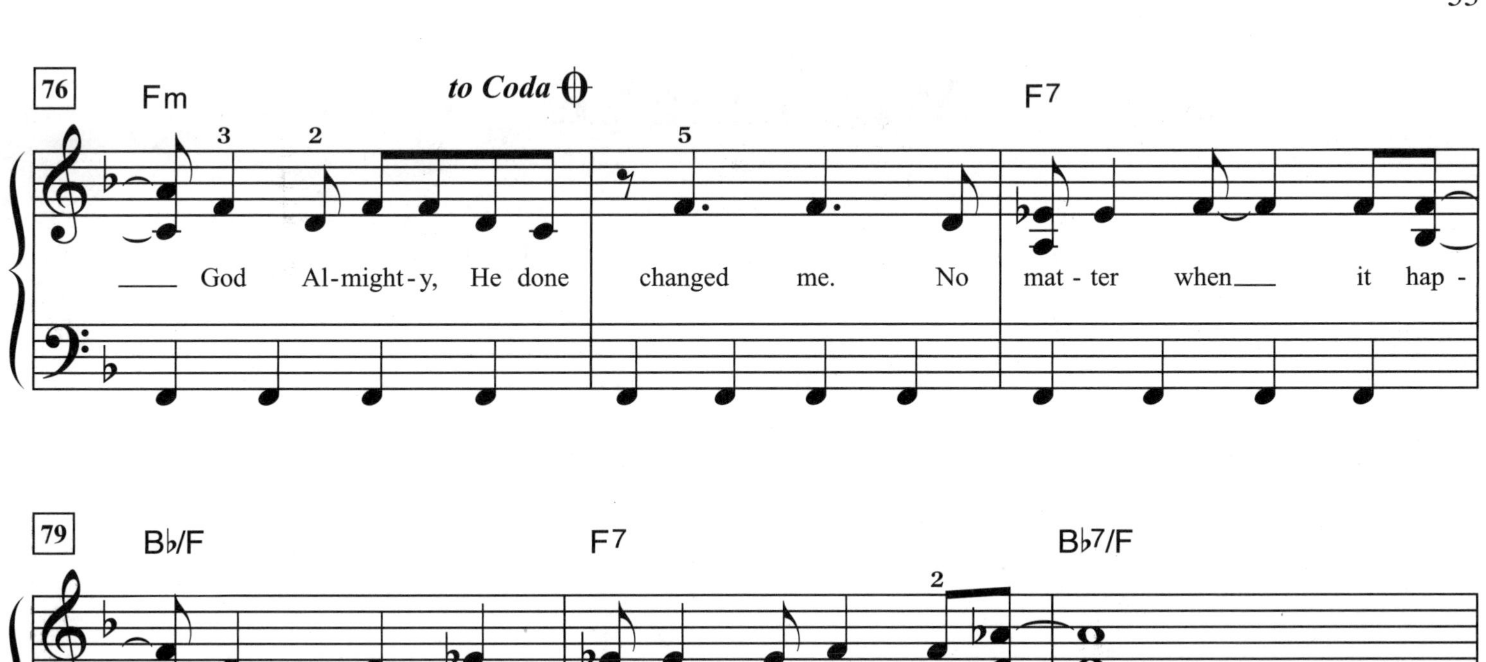

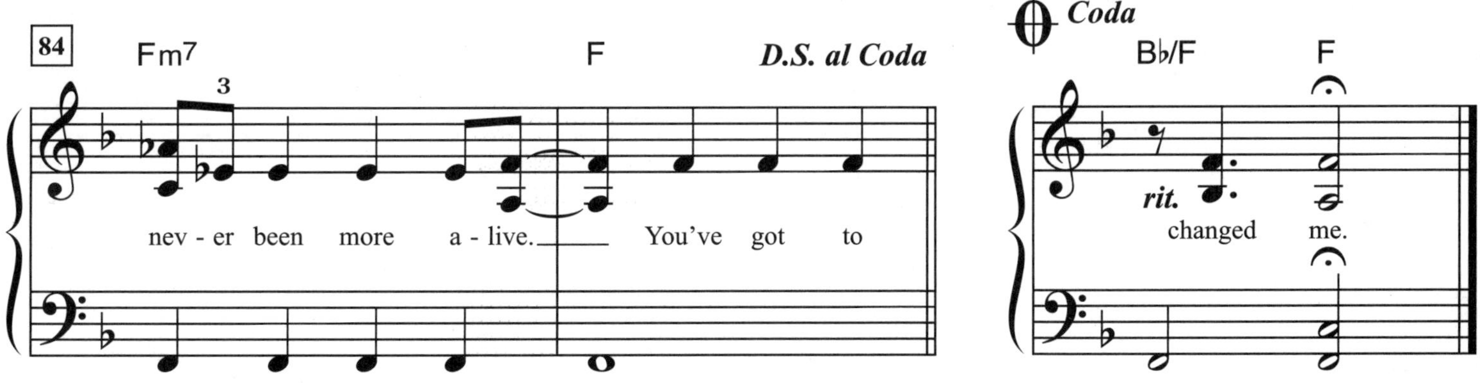

Verse 2:
Maybe He came to you when everything seemed fine,
Or maybe your world was upside down,
It hit you right between the eye, eye, eyes.
No matter when it happened, at seven or ninety-five,
Move your feet, 'cause you are free,
And you've never been more alive.

WE BELIEVE

Words and Music by Matthew Hooper,
Richie Fike and Travis Ryan
Arr. Carol Tornquist

Verse:
13
D
G/D
D
In this bro - ken gen-e - ra - tion
when all is dark, You help us
16
G/D
Bm7
see.
There is on - ly one sal -
18
G
D
G/D
va - tion:
we be-lieve,
we be-lieve.
mf
We be-lieve
Chorus:
21
D
Asus
in God the Fath - er,
we be-lieve
in Je - sus Christ.
We be-lieve
23
Bm
G
in the Ho - ly Spir - it,
and He's
giv - en us
new life.
We be-lieve

25
D
Asus
in the Cru - ci - fix - ion, we be-lieve that He con-quered death. We be-lieve
27
Bm
G
in the Res - ur - rec - tion and He's com-ing back a - gain. We be-lieve.
29
D
G/D
mp
2. So,
Verse:
31
D
G/D
let our faith be more than an - thems,
33
D
G/D
great - er than the songs we sing.

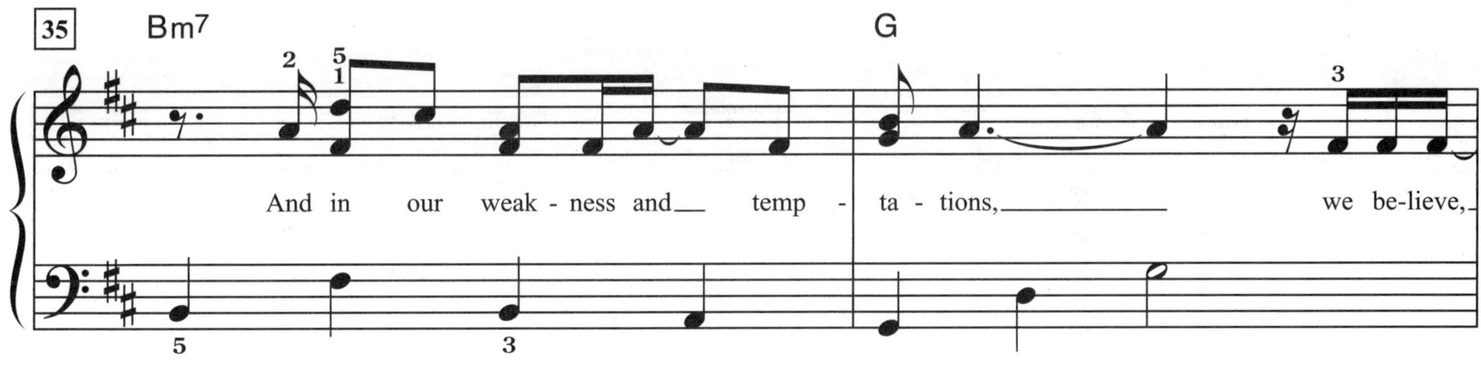
35
Bm7
G
2
5
1
3
And in our weak - ness and temp - ta - tions, we be-lieve,
5
3

37
D
G/D
5
we be-lieve.
mf
We be-lieve

Chorus:
39
D
Asus
in God the Fa - ther, we be-lieve in Je - sus Christ. We be-lieve
2

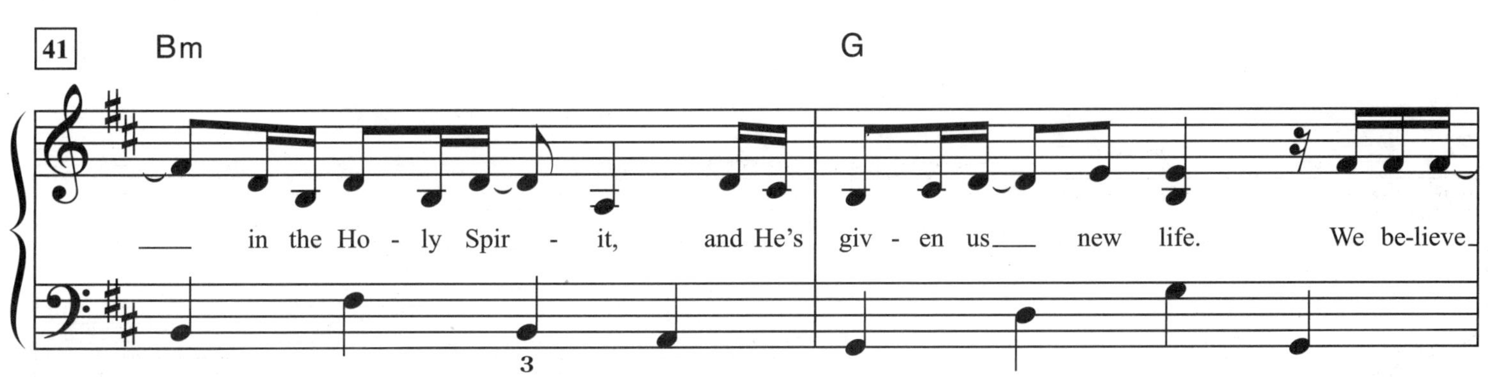
41
Bm
G
in the Ho - ly Spir - it, and He's giv - en us new life. We be-lieve
3

43
D
Asus
in the Cru - ci - fix - ion, we be-lieve that He con-quered death. We be-lieve

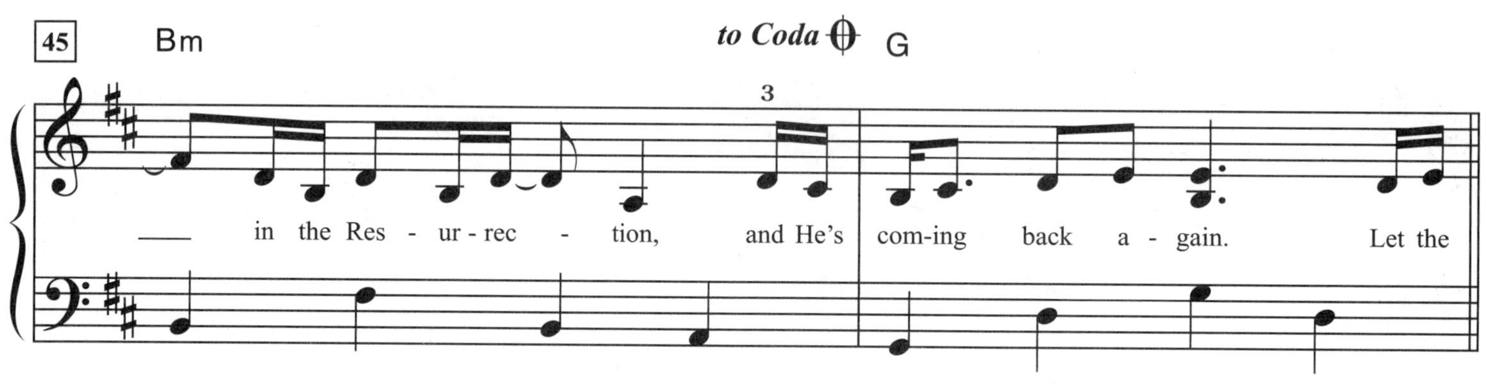
45
Bm
to Coda
G
in the Res - ur - rec - tion, and He's com-ing back a - gain. Let the

Bridge:

47
G
Asus
Bm7
D/A
lost be found and the dead be raised, in the here and now, let love in-vade. Let the

49
G
Asus
Bm7
D/A
church live loud. Our God, we'll say, "We be-lieve! We be - lieve!" And the

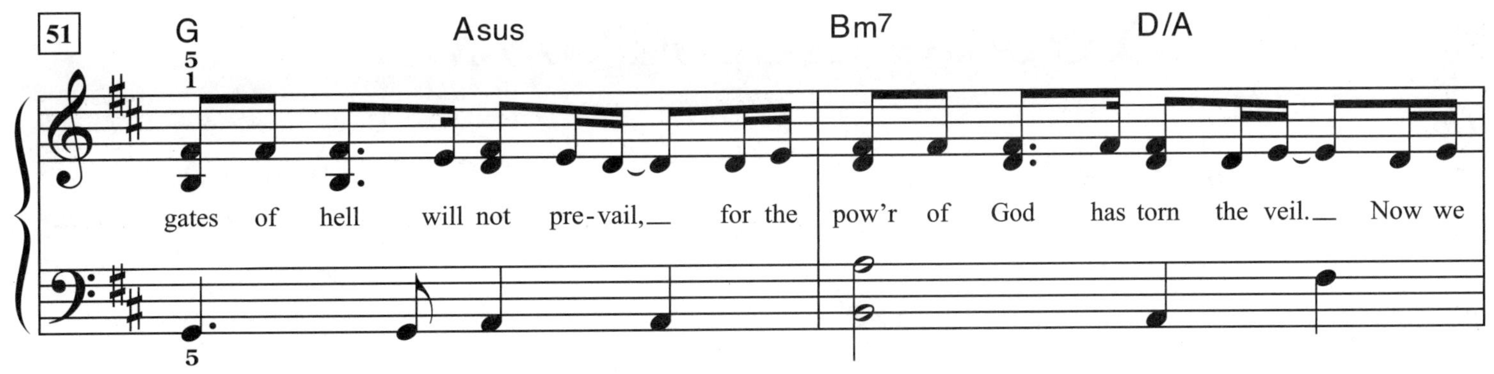
51
G
Asus
Bm7
D/A
gates of hell will not pre-vail, for the pow'r of God has torn the veil. Now we

D.S. al Coda
53
G
Asus
Bm7
D/A
know Your love will nev - er fail. We be-lieve, we be-lieve. We be-lieve

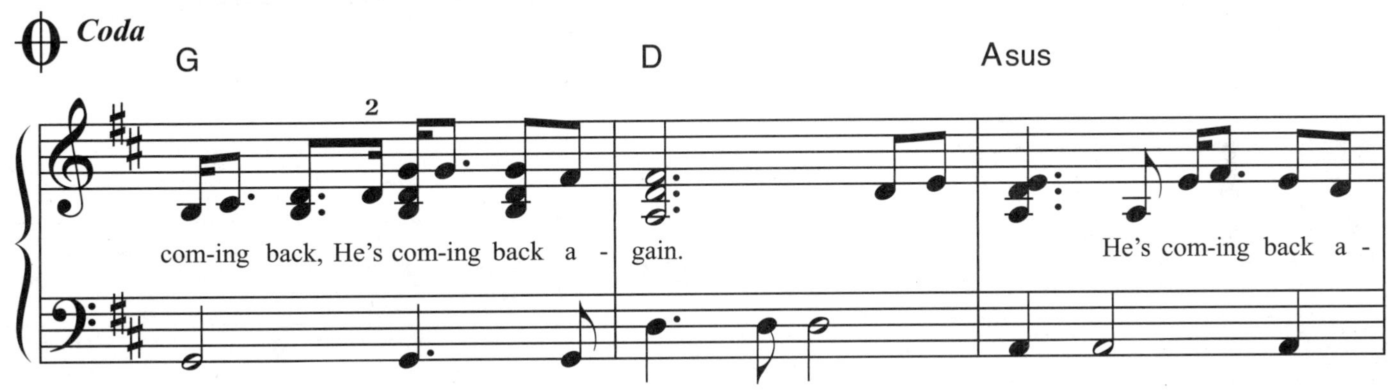
Coda
G
D
Asus
com-ing back, He's com-ing back a - gain. He's com-ing back a -

58
Bm7
G
gain.
rit. e dim.
We be-lieve, we be-lieve.
mp

YOUR GRACE FINDS ME

Words and Music by
Jonas Myrin and Matt Redman
Arr. Carol Tornquist

14
E♭
B♭
there in the ev - 'ry - day and the mun - dane,
same for the saint and for the sin - ner,
16
E♭
F/A
Gm
F
there in the sor-row and the danc-ing, Your great grace, oh, such
e-nough for this whole wide world, Your great grace, oh, such
Chorus:
19
E♭
to Coda
B♭
grace.
grace.
mf
From the cre-a - tion to the cross,
22
Gm
E♭
B♭/D
E♭
then from the cross in - to e - ter - ni-ty, Your grace finds me,
25
B♭
D.S. al Coda
yes, Your grace finds me.

Chorus 2:
Coda
B♭
Gm
There in the dark-est night of the soul,
there in the sweet-est songs of
31
E♭
B♭/D
E♭
vic - to-ry, Your grace finds me,
yes, Your grace
34
B♭
F
finds me.
Your great
grace,
oh, such
37
E♭
F
E♭
grace,
Your great
grace,
oh, such
grace.
40
mp
B♭
E♭/B♭

44
B♭
E♭/B♭
B♭
E♭/B♭
48
B♭
E♭/B♭
B♭
E♭/B♭
So, I'm
52
B♭
E♭/B♭
breath - ing in Your grace, and I'm breath - ing out Your praise. I'm
54
B♭
1.
E♭/B♭
2.
E♭/B♭
breath-ing in Your grace. For - ev - er I'll be For - ev - er I'll be.
57
E♭
B♭
rit. e dim.
Your grace finds me.
p

THIS IS AMAZING GRACE

Words and Music by Jeremy Riddle,
Phil Wickham and Joshua Neil Farro
Arr. Carol Tornquist

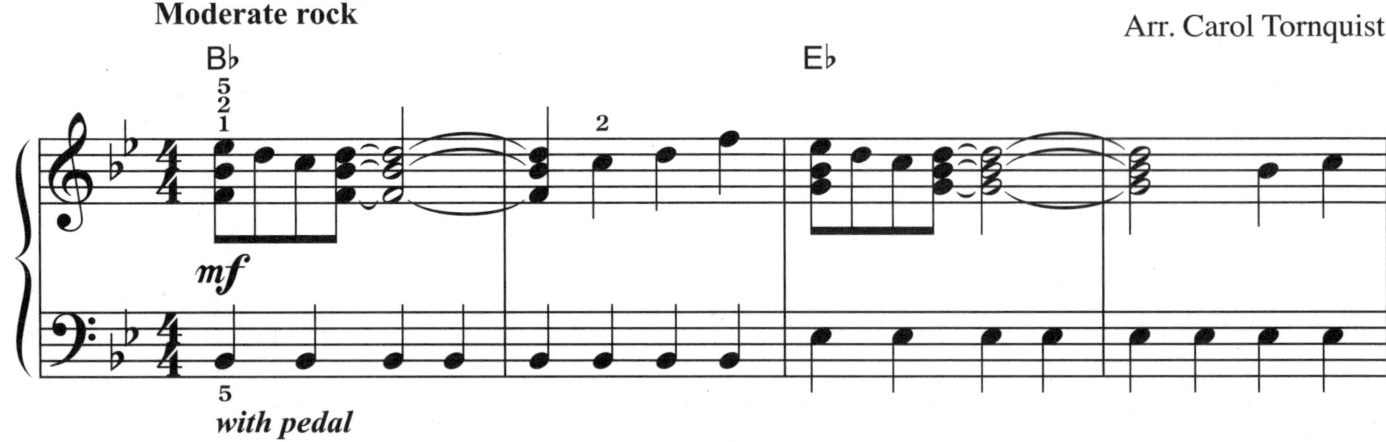

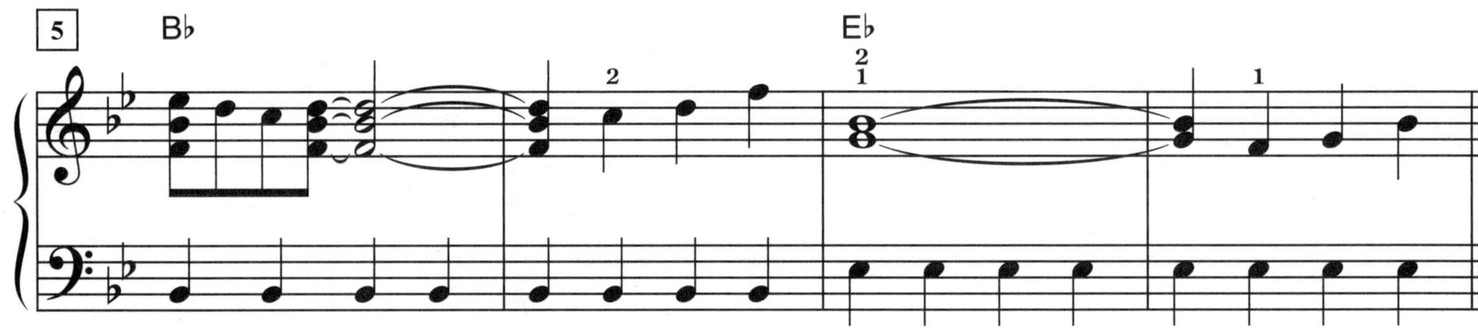

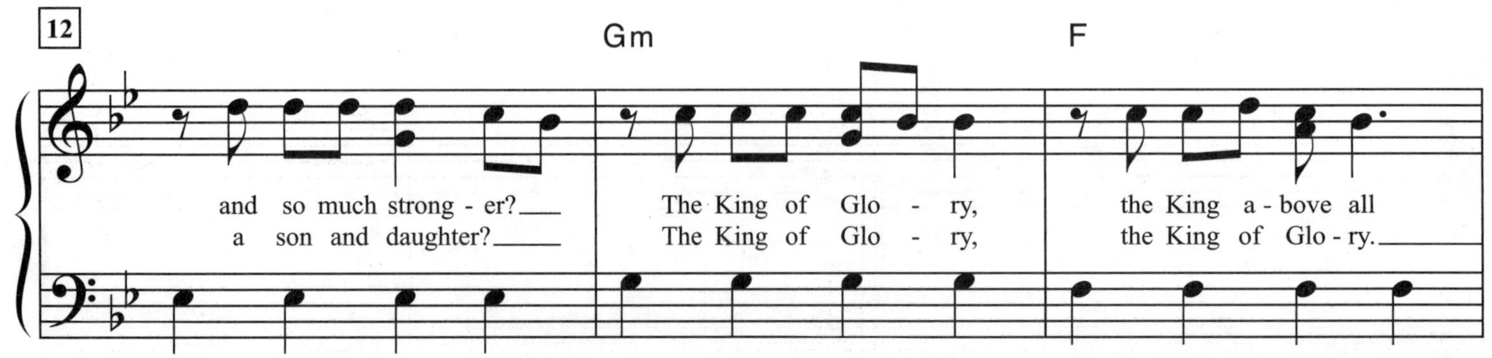

15
E♭
B♭
kings.
Who shakes the whole earth
Who rules the na - tions

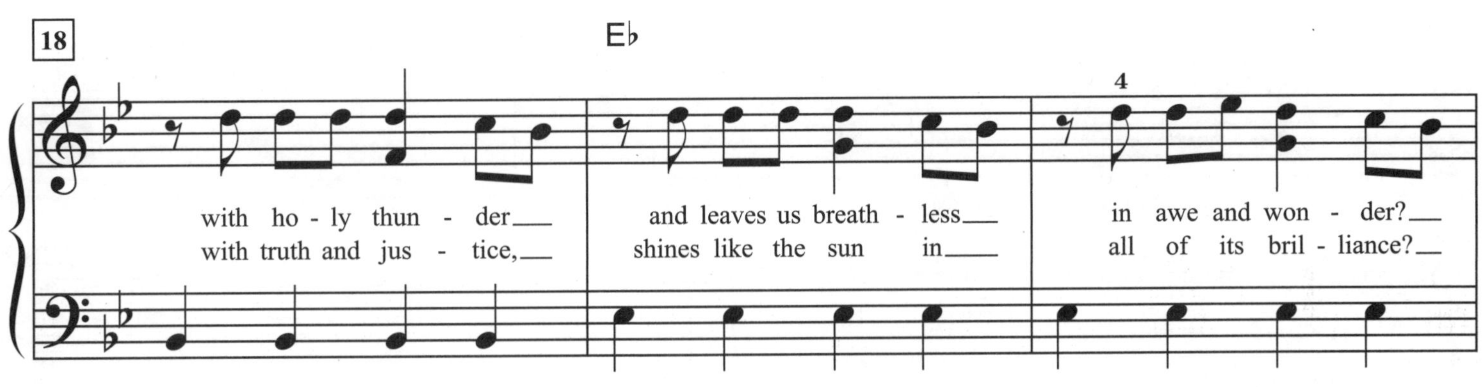
18
E♭
with ho - ly thun - der
with truth and jus - tice,
and leaves us breath - less
shines like the sun in
in awe and won - der?
all of its bril - liance?

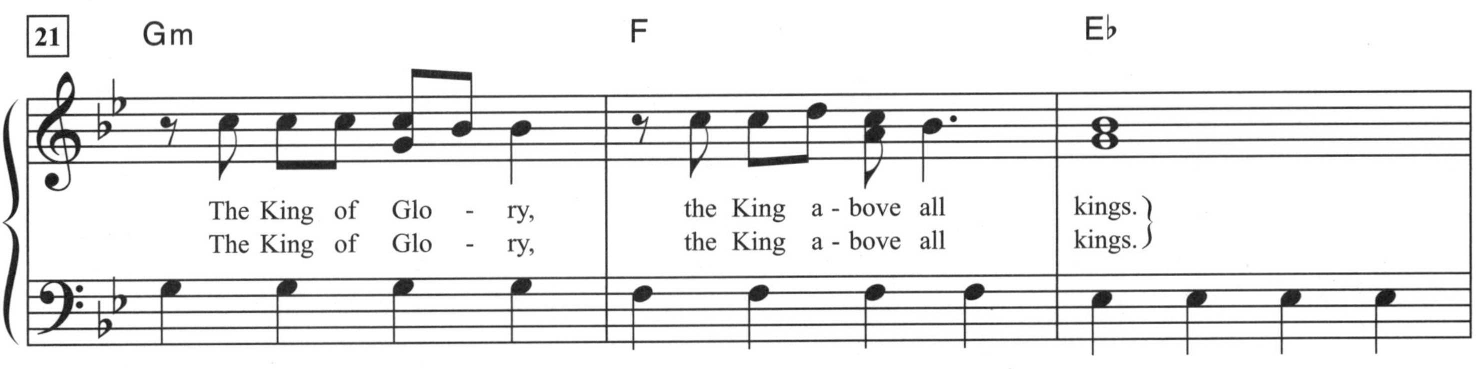
21
Gm
F
E♭
The King of Glo - ry,
The King of Glo - ry,
the King a - bove all
the King a - bove all
kings.
kings.

Chorus:
24
B♭
This is a - maz - ing grace,
this is un - fail - ing love,

27
E♭
Gm7
5
that You would take my place,

30
F
4
3
that You would bear my cross.
You laid down Your life

33
B♭
E♭
4
4
that I would be set free.

36
Gm
1.
F
4
Oh
Je - sus, I sing for
all that You've done for

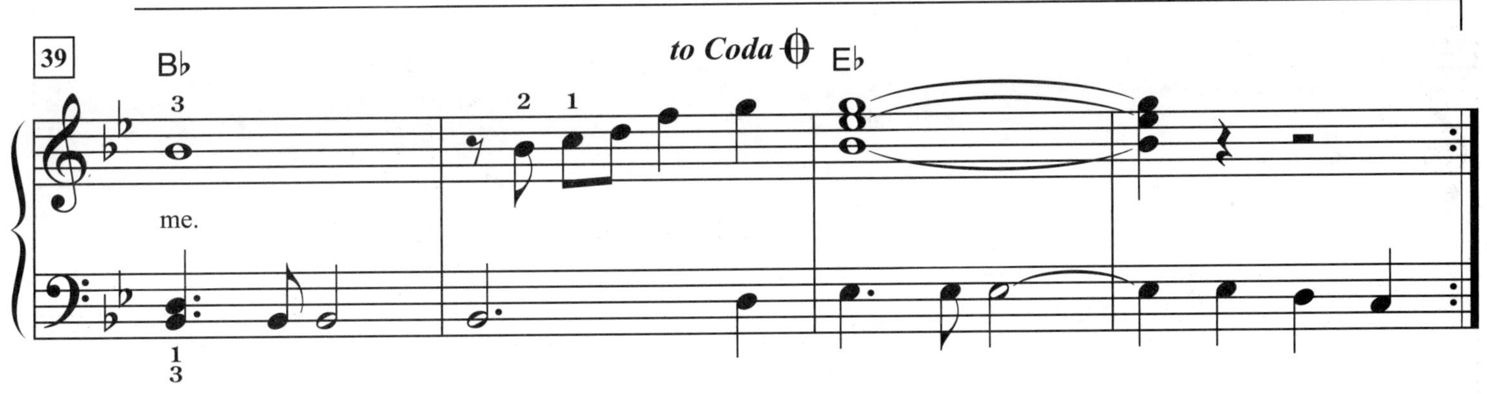
39
B♭
to Coda
E♭
me.

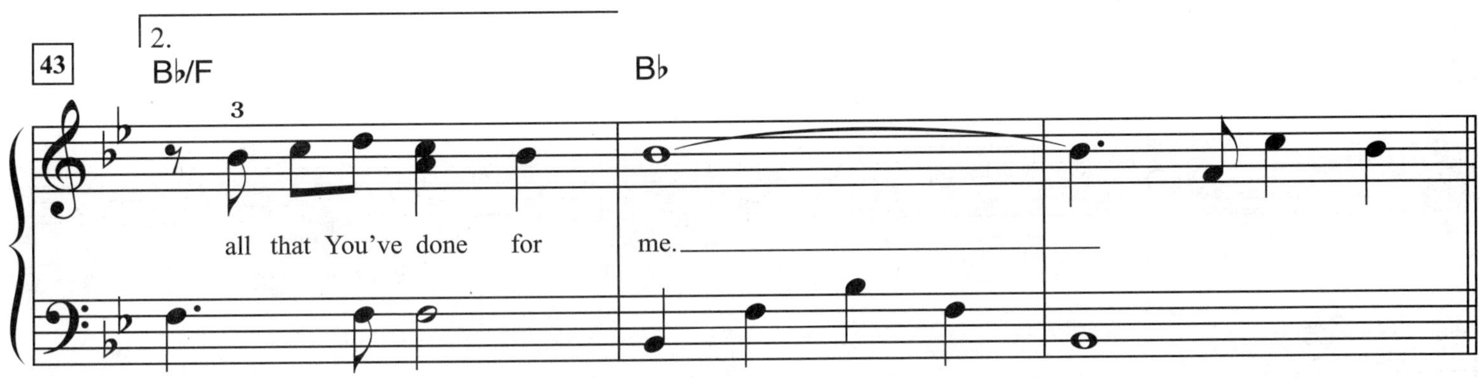
2.
43
B♭/F
B♭
all that You've done for
me.

Bridge:

46
B♭
E♭
Wor - thy is the Lamb who was slain.
Wor - thy is the King who con -

49
B♭
quered the grave.
Wor - thy is the Lamb who was slain,

52
E♭
B♭
Wor-thy is the King who has con - quered the grave.
Wor-thy is the Lamb who was slain.

55
E♭
Wor-thy is the King who has con - quered the grave.

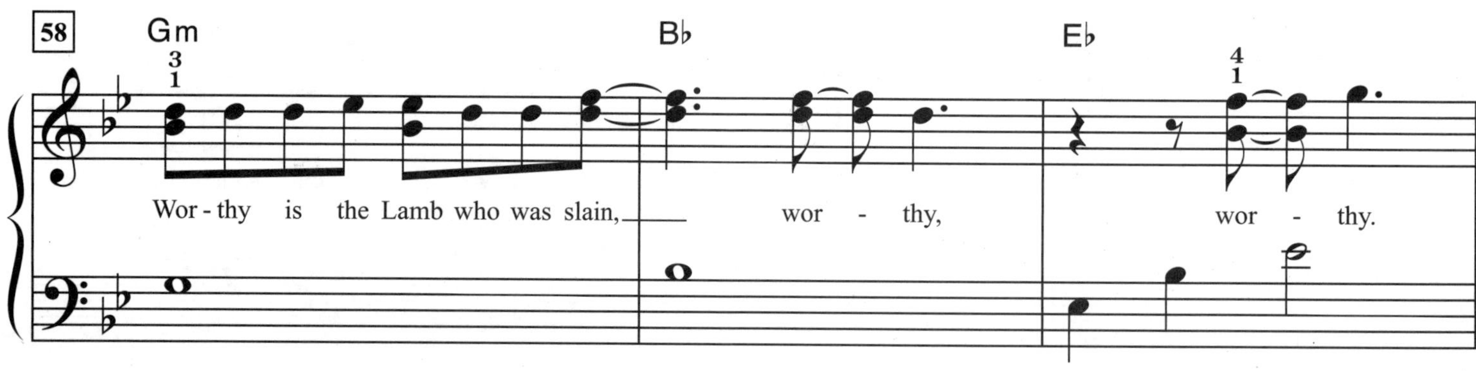
58
Gm
B♭
E♭
Wor-thy is the Lamb who was slain,
wor - thy,
wor - thy.

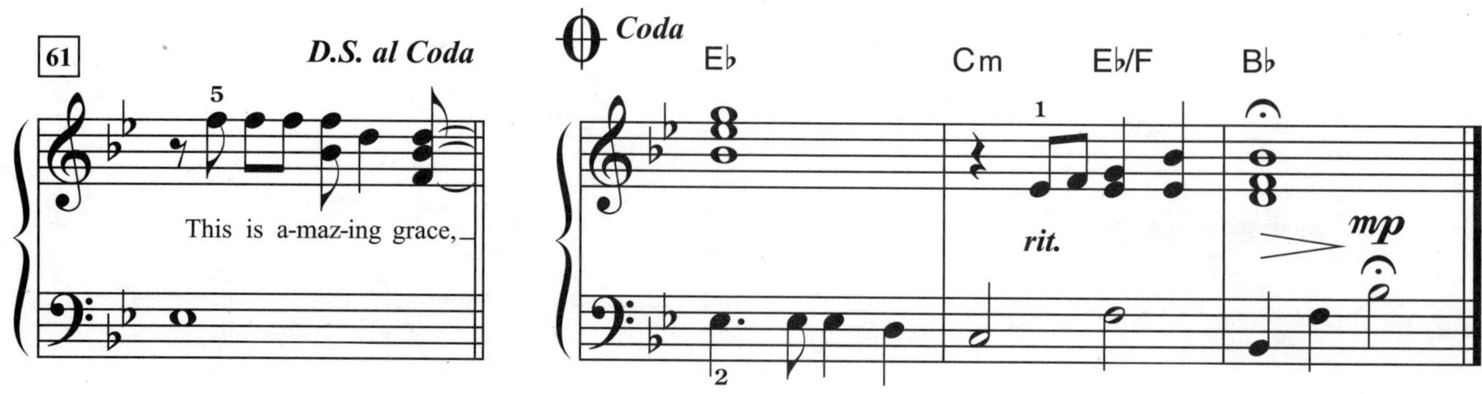
61
D.S. al Coda
Coda
E♭
Cm
E♭/F
B♭
This is a-maz-ing grace,
rit.
mp